GOYA

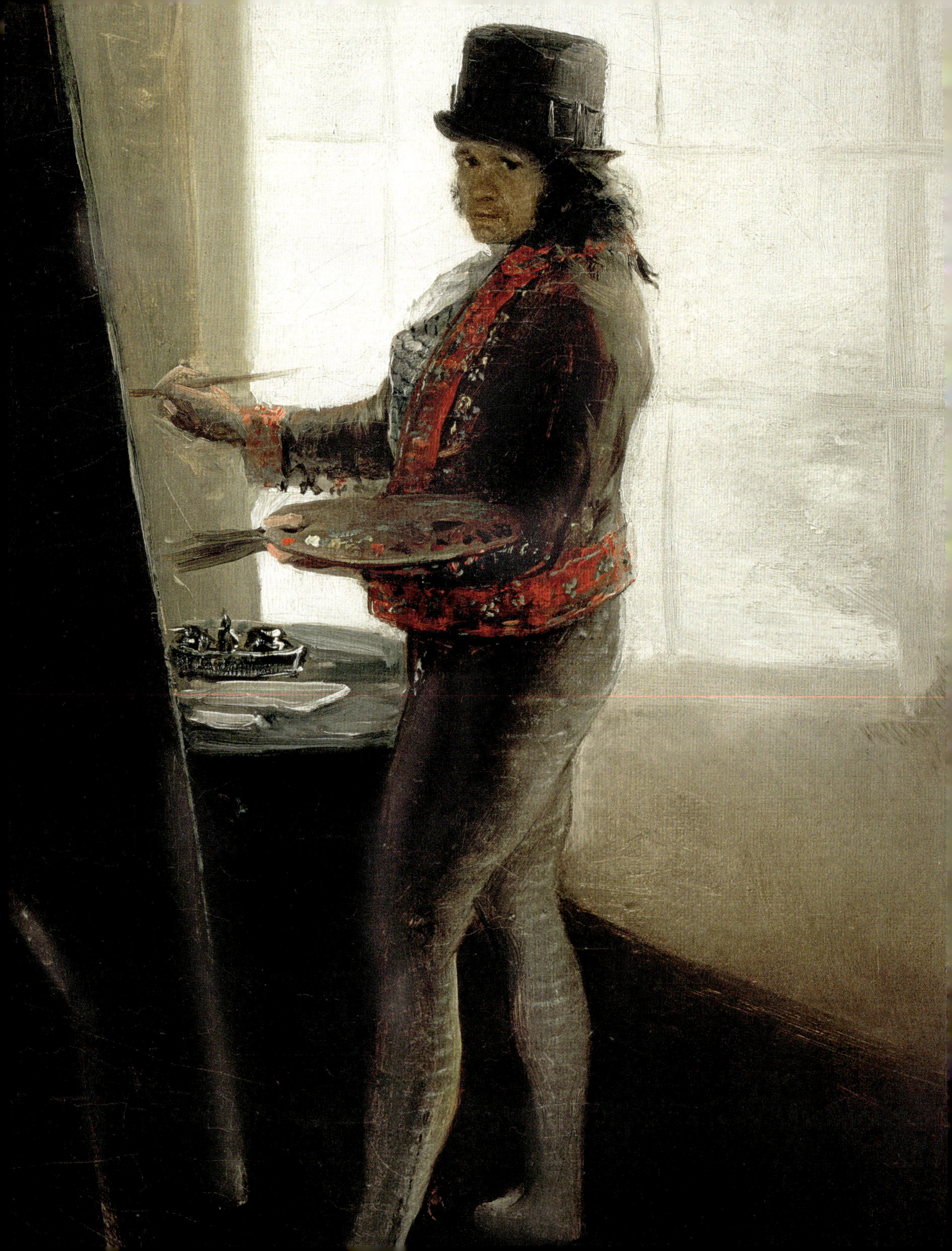

MASTERS OF ART

GOYA

Jacqueline Cockburn

PRESTEL

Munich · London · New York

Front Cover: Francisco José Goya, *The Parasol*, c. 1777 (detail, pages 12/13)

Frontispiece: Francisco José Goya, *Self-Portrait in the Studio*, 1794/95 (pages 60/61)

© Prestel Verlag, Munich · London · New York 2025
A member of Penguin Random House Verlagsgruppe GmbH
Neumarkter Strasse 28 · 81673 Munich

produktsicherheit@penguinrandomhouse.de

A CIP catalogue record for this book is available from the British Library.

Editorial direction, Prestel: Cornelia Hübler
Copyediting and proofreading: Vanessa Magson-Mann, So to Speak, Icking
Production management: Martina Effaga
Design: Florian Frohnholzer, Sofarobotnik
Typesetting: ew print & media service gmbh
Separations: Reproline mediateam
Printing and binding: Pixartprinting, Lavis
Typeface: Cera Pro
Paper: 150 g/m² Magno Matt

Penguin Random House Verlagsgruppe FSC® N001967

Printed in Italy

ISBN 978-3-7913-9375-9

www.prestel.com

CONTENTS

INTRODUCTION

Francisco José Goya, from provincial origins to First Court Painter, has become one of the best-known Spanish artists of all time. He straddles the eighteenth and nineteenth centuries and is difficult to categorise. Adventurous Academic? Cynical Romantic? Closet Humanist? Dramatic Realist? Funny, engaging and morose. Goya was born at a time when the Industrial Revolution was about to usher changes in the lives of people in the rest of Europe while Spain faced political and social upheaval and was not to modernise for many years. The painter was both old-school and innovative at the same time. Whether we are looking at old crones, flying witches, bullfighters in the ring, angels or demons, we are transported to other worlds by this extraordinary Aragonese artist who spent most of his working life at the court of Spain in Madrid, kowtowing to the aristocrats, bowing to the monarchy and scraping to the Intelligentsia.

To what can we attribute his meteoric rise? A father who was a gilder and had the ear of the artistic milieu of Zaragoza? A capacity to spot an opportunity? An ability to capture the turmoil of the time or perhaps more accurately a simply marvellous brushstroke? Goya lathers his canvases with sweeping, thickly laid strokes of paint, with a confidence in his own brilliance, capturing a crooked smile or a leering grin, an arrogant gaze or a sensual stare. Men and women, with all their fascinating foibles are rendered with a determination to seek the truth. Goya saw war and was able to convey the true horror not just of those who died at gunpoint, but those who were strung up, stripped bare to die with no dignity or were bludgeoned to death. He saw war, as he saw a bullfight—as a mortal, relentless and bloody combat. Yet his softer renditions of naked beauty and pale fragility point to a man whose sensitivity meant he understood suffering.

It is not known exactly how he went deaf, but it is known that he lived in a silent world for nearly three decades during which he and his wife lost countless children while he managed life at court. Capricious, spoilt and often ineffective kings and queens came and went, along with their advisers. One often wonders how Goya stayed under the radar of a terrorising Inquisition which would be abolished soon after his death. Through his letters, mostly to and from his oldest friend Martín

Zapater, we know he loved chocolate, snuff, 'roscones' (round doughnuts) shooting, fishing and music before he went deaf, but we do not know how he felt about his wife or whether he loved the beautiful Duchess of Alba and despised the royals he worked for.

So much of Goya's life is shrouded in mystery and contradictions. Did he absorb the thoughts of the enlightened aristocracy, or enjoy a caper with street musicians, or did he share a prayer with men and women on a pilgrimage? Did he side with those who read Voltaire, if they could get their hands on the books, or with those whose endeavours led them to more religious pursuits? Ultimately, there is the extraordinary number of paintings, drawings, etchings, prints and frescoes to pour over and we must make our own decisions.

Goya looked to Velázquez for inspiration and he himself inspired later artists. When Edouard Manet went to the Prado in 1865, he marvelled at Goya and darkened his own brushstroke. He copied shamelessly and reinvented Goya's energy in his own *The Execution of Maximilian* (1867/68) or *Olympia* (1863). Are those Frances Bacon's distorted faces lurking in the so-called *Black Paintings* that Seamus Heaney loved and Joan Miró admired so much? Many were inspired by Goya. The Spanish composer Enrique Granados wrote the *Goyescas* in 1911, an evocative suite for piano, then a later opera. Novels, poems, countless films and even video games have been based on Goya's works. Goya seems to live on through Picasso's adherence to black and white in *Guernica* and to his rendition of the horrors of a later civil war. When Dinos and Jake Chapman bought and subsequently defaced one of Goya's series of *The Disasters of War* we cannot help but wonder whether he might just have approved.

Illness and political turbulence did not dampen the artist's spirits and he lived to the ripe old age of eighty-two and died in Bordeaux. His works can be seen in galleries and museums all over the world. Goya helped to spread the myth of a Black Spain which was held back by an overwhelming Church, a cruel Inquisition, despotic monarchs and selfish politicians, and yet his vibrant greens, velvet reds and lemon yellows adorn our gallery walls and bring us joy.

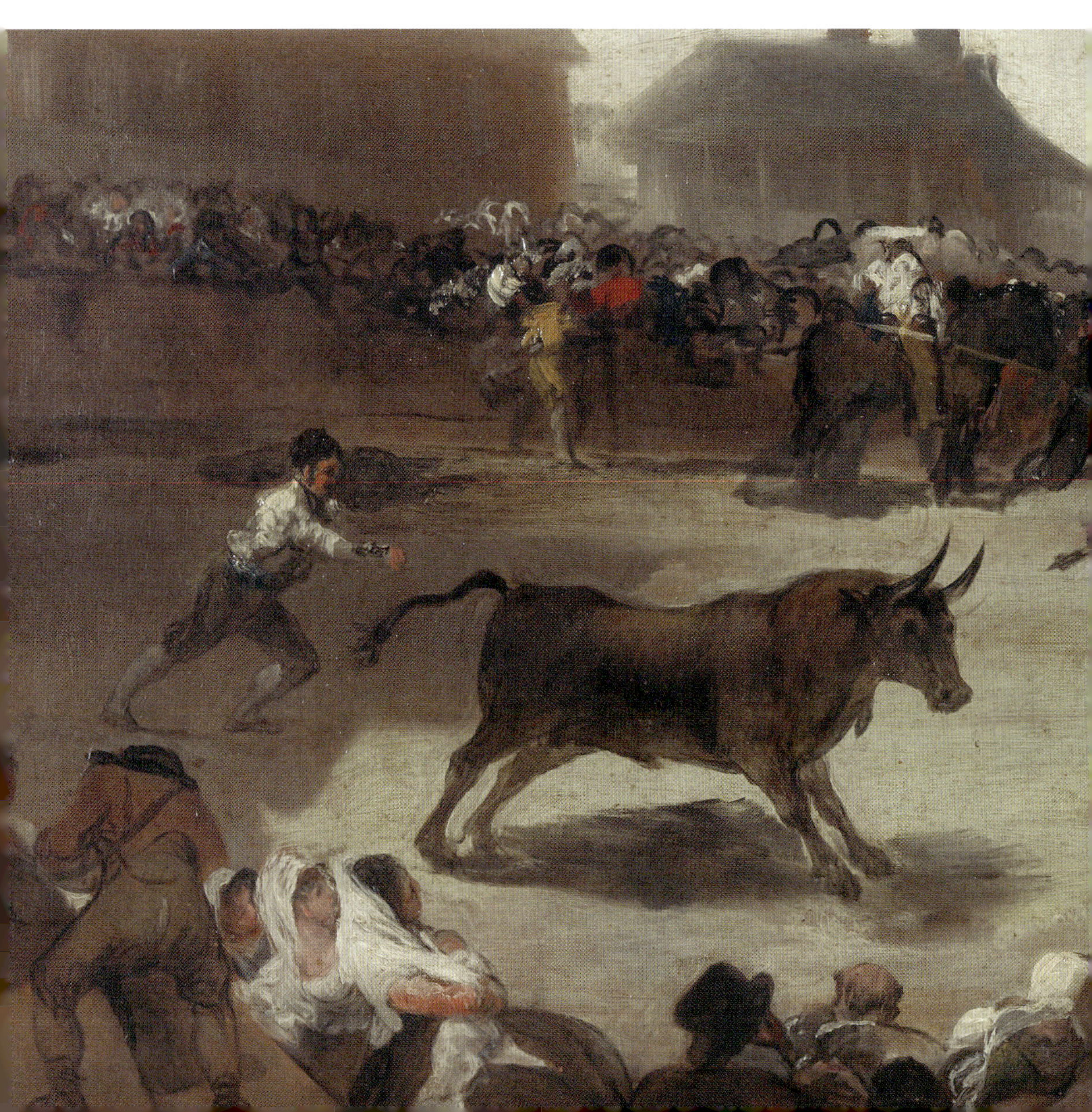

LIFE

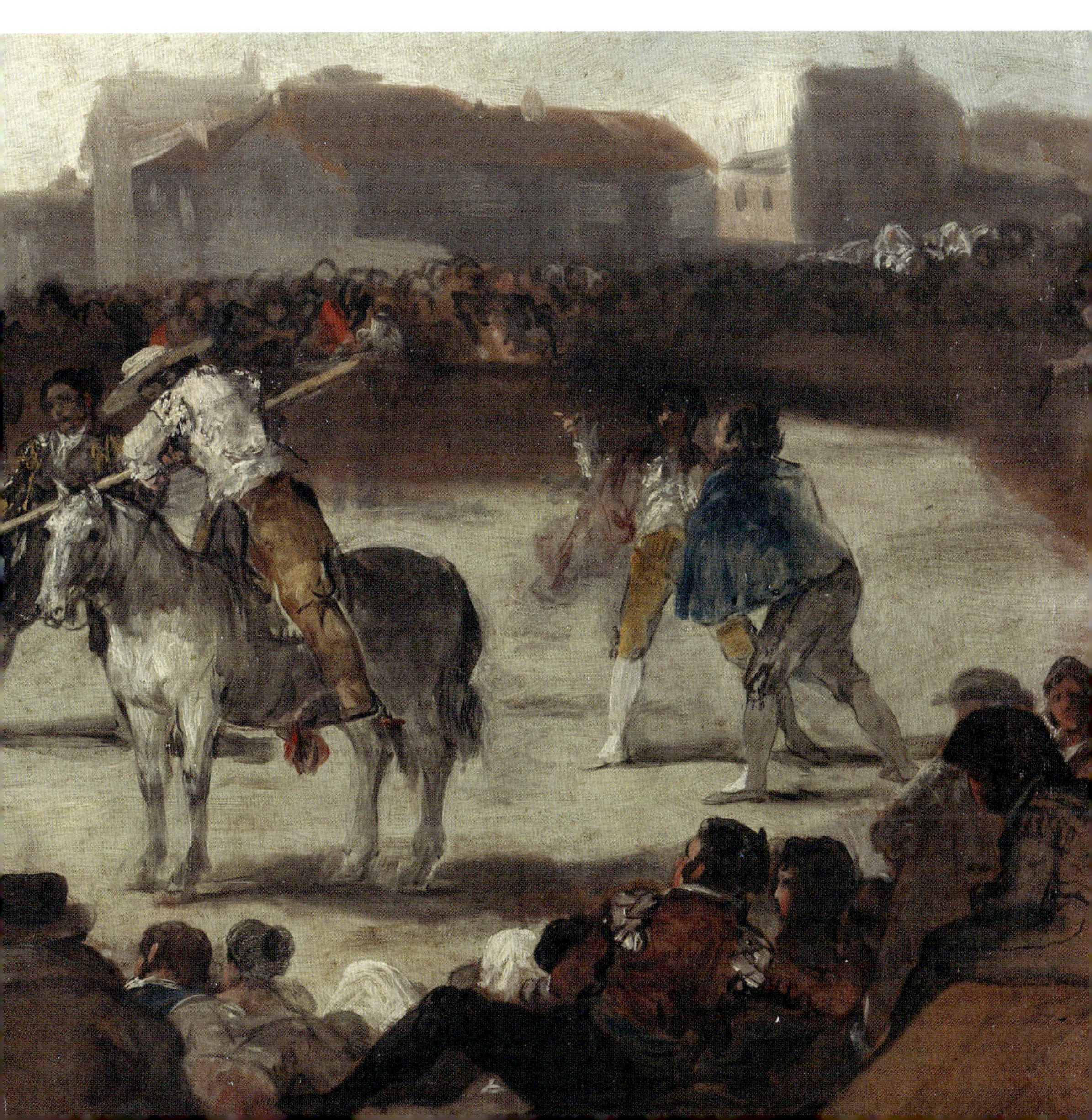

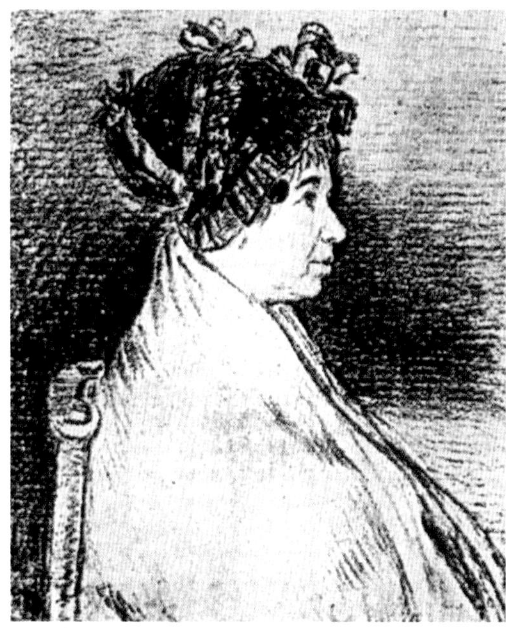

Josefa Bayeu, 1805

Francisco José de Goya y Lucientes—subversive and satirical social climber, revolutionary, liberal thinker, fiercely loyal, scurrilous fourth child of the gilder, Braulio José and his wife Gracia Lucientes, was born in a tiny stone house in the riverless, bleak hill-top village of Fuentetodos, Spain, on 30 March 1746. He was baptised in the small local church San Gil, built in 1724 with stones from a ruined castle and adorned with an altarpiece gilded by his father. Within a month of his birth the family moved some sixty-five kilometres away to the larger city of Zaragoza, also in the municipality of Aragon, where Goya lived for most of his childhood. The family was lower middle class, proud of the grandfather who was a notary which gave them a certain social standing. It is thought that Goya attended a church school run by Piarist Fathers, which is where he possibly met his lifelong friend and recipient of over a hundred and forty letters—Martín Zapater.

Goya's father had some success during his life and was put in charge of gilding the sanctuary of the principal church of Zaragoza, Santa María del Pilar. This exposed his thirteen-year-old young son to artists for the first time and, by the age of fourteen, the precocious Goya applied for a bursary at the San Fernando Royal Academy of Fine Arts in Madrid which he failed to achieve, but, due to his father's connections with the influential brothers Francisco and Ramón Bayeu, Goya was apprenticed to José Luzán y Martinez, artist and reviewer of paintings for the Inquisition. Luzán, who had studied in Naples, set up an Academy in Zaragoza where, from 1760 onwards, Goya studied for four years learning design and print copying. This experience and the help of the Pignatelli family paved the way for Goya to study in Italy between 1770 and 1771 and learn the styles of painting so revered by the Spanish court. A short time later, on 25 July 1773 in the parish church of San Martín, he married María Josefa Bayeu ('Pepa'), the sister of the important Bayeu brothers and most notably Francisco Bayeu, who was a senior court painter. That fact must have been a dou-ble-edged sword for the ambitious Goya. Little is known about Pepa other than her sad history of numerous pregnancies, with only one child, Javier, surviving into maturity.

Eighteenth-century Spain was a time of con-fusion, progress and fear. Teetering nervously on the edge of the Enlightenment, it was rigor-ously and ruthlessly dominated by the enemies

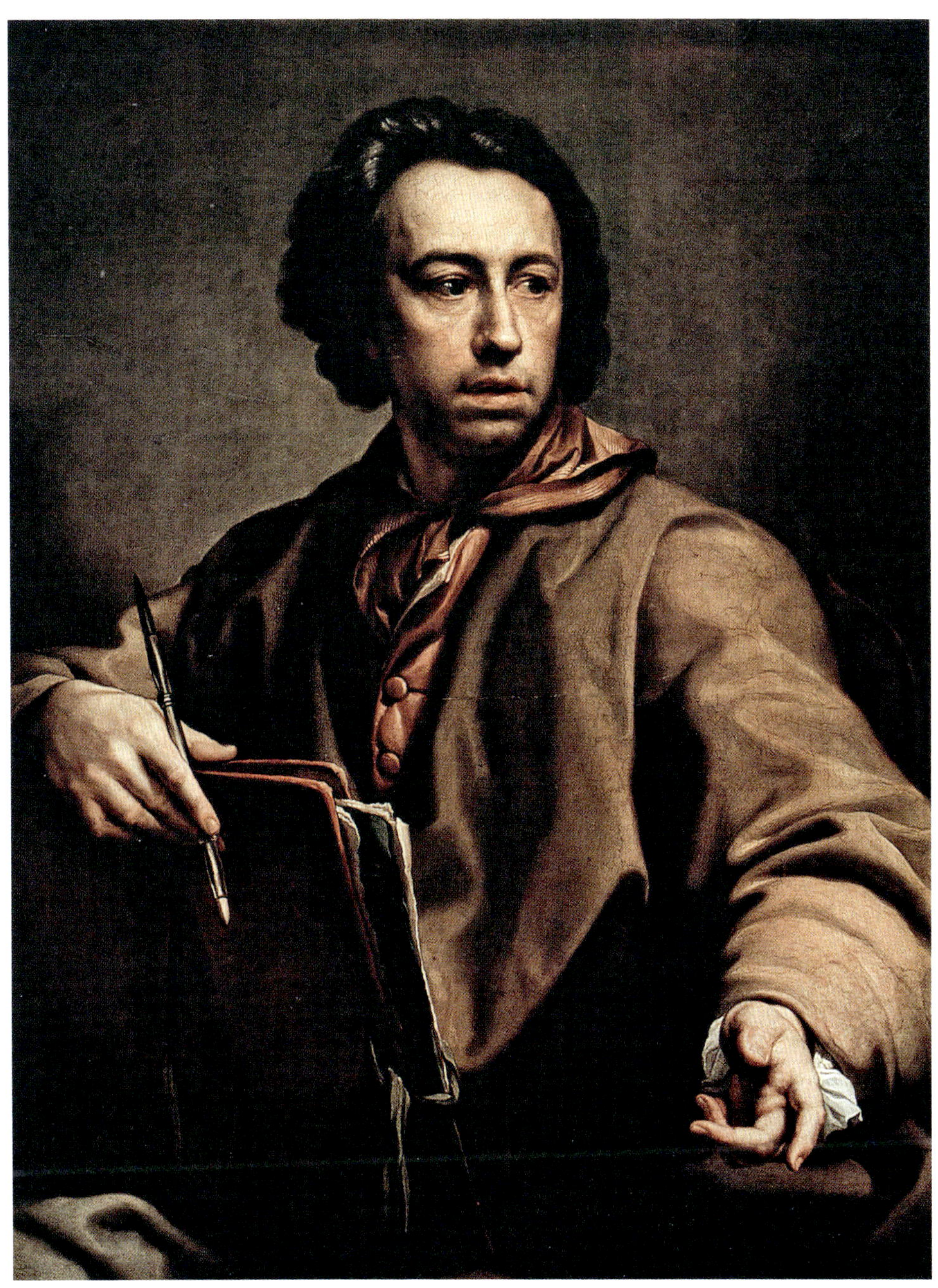

Anton Raphael Mengs, *Self-Portrait*, c. 1775

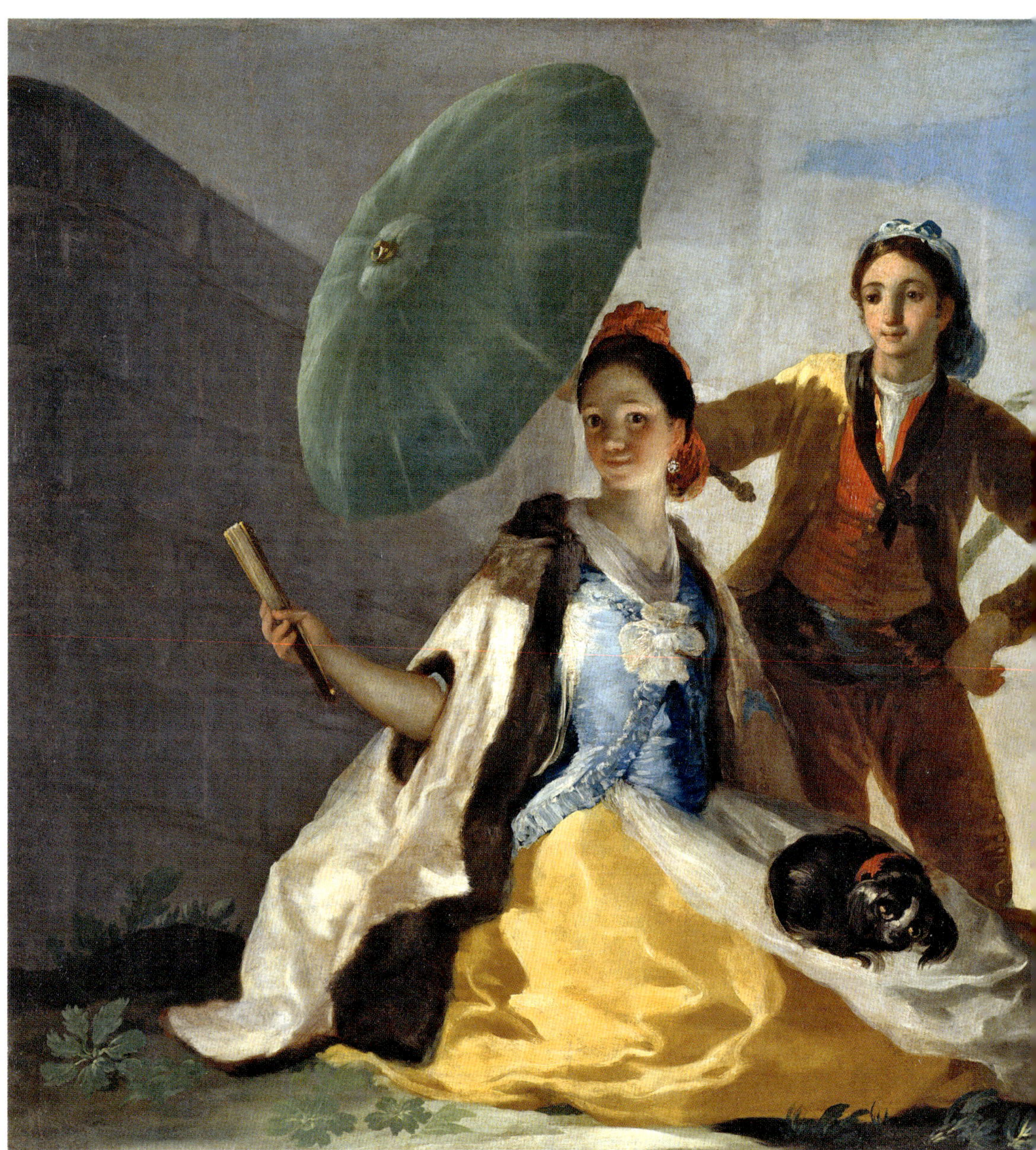

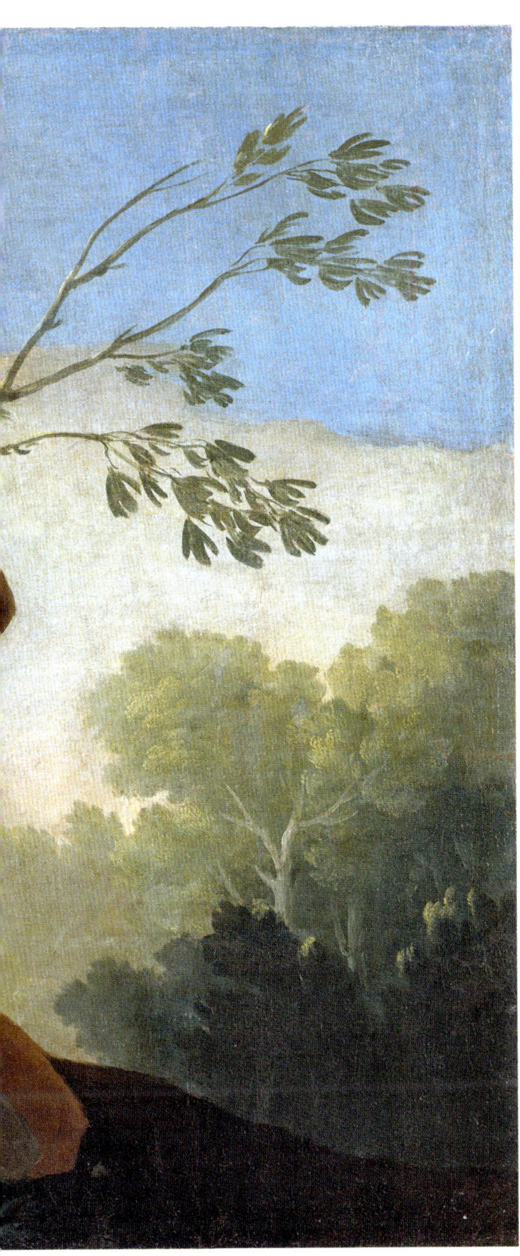

of progressive thinking—the church and the Inquisition. Spain, once the most important European empire, had suffered humiliating losses of territory. Its heirless royal family, the Hapsburgs, had ended their reign at the dawn of the century provoking a war of succession and the installation of the noble French Bourbon family as kings of Spain. Subsequent Spanish Bourbon kings would play a large part in the life of the once provincial Goya.

By 1772 the artist had completed his first church commission—to paint frescoes on sacred subjects for the Church of Santa María del Pilar in Zaragoza. He would return to these frescoes in 1780 when he was elected to an honorary position at the San Fernando Royal Academy of Fine Arts. A later important commission would take him to a Carthusian Monastery, the Aula Dei, where he made a series of murals applying oils directly onto the plaster. They were on the subject of the life of the Virgin and painted high up on the nave of the presbytery walls. They sadly fell into disrepair and had to be painted over later. By 3 January 1775 Goya set off to Madrid and, through the influence of his brothers-in-law, began working at the Royal Tapestry Factory of Santa Barbara where he would eventually become director in 1777. Tapestries designed by Goya and made for the royal family to warm and decorate their palaces brought him the attention of the Bourbon court, cementing a patronage that would continue for the rest of his life.

Although he would eventually tire of tapestry work which was not prestigious, it is here, following in the footsteps of some of the great figures

LA S. D MARIA TERESA
HIJA DEL SER. INFANTE
D. LUIS
DE EDAD DE DOS AÑOS Y NUEVE MESES

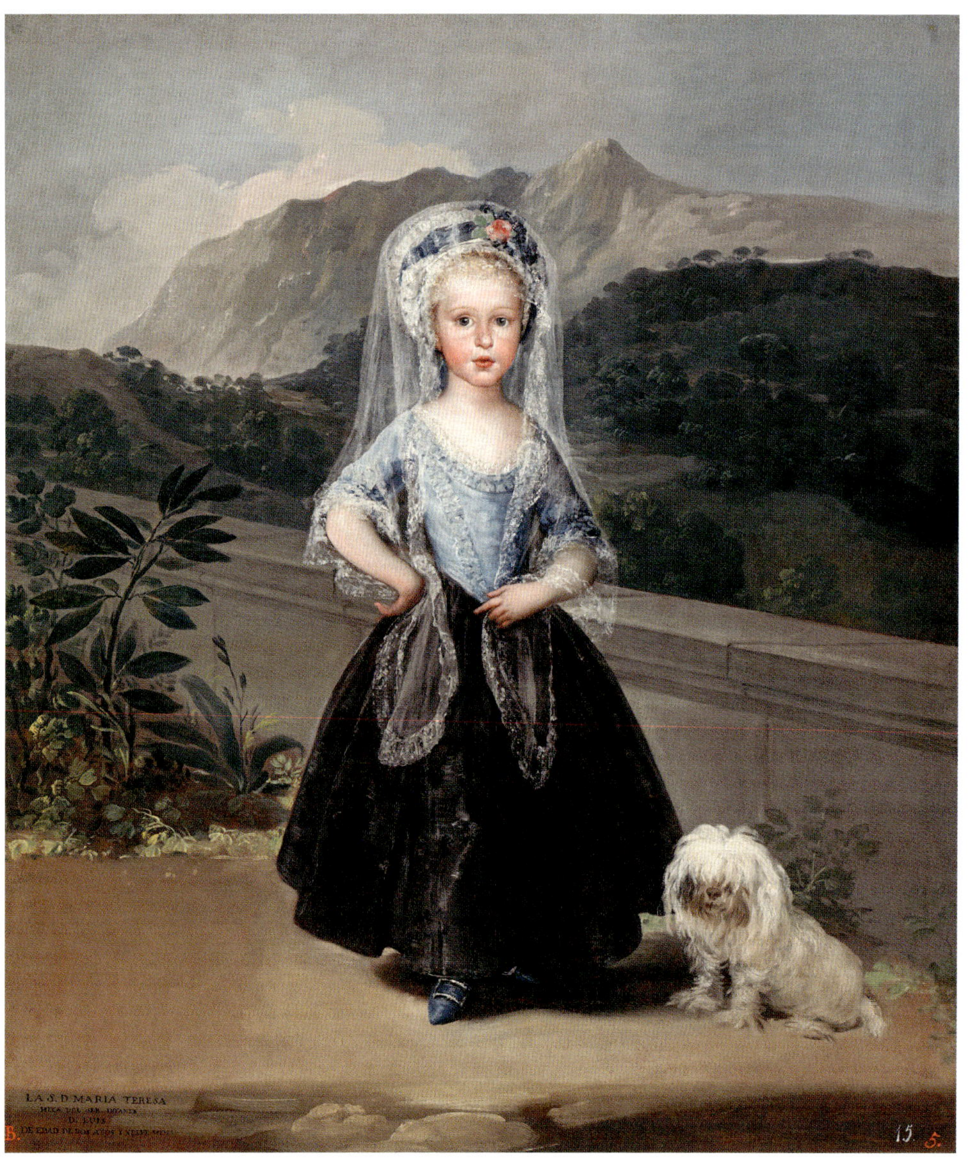

14

of Spanish Literature: Cervantes, Quevedo, Tirso de Molina, Góngora and San Juan de la Cruz, that he would begin to create archetypal characters from Spanish life. He had the support of the court painter—Anton Raphael Mengs (page 11), a highly regarded artist of the time who, having been summoned by King Charles III from Italy in 1761, had brought Goya's brother-in-law, Francisco Bayeu, to court as his assistant. Finally, Goya had exposure to royal circles. He would absorb the Spanish culture of *sainetes*, popular comic operas and invent his own *majos* and *majas*, who were representatives of the popular classes and streets of Madrid. For Goya, invention was everything. For seventeen years he captured the stock characters and heroes of Spanish and sometimes foreign literature; picnics à la Watteau, colourful scenes à la Tiepolo, snapshots of urban life with street vendors, musicians and festivals. He observed weddings and courting rituals, clearly enjoying capturing cultural mores of the time and being in tune with the people as can be seen in paintings such as the one of a foppishly dressed young man holding an umbrella to shield a coquettish woman from the hot Spanish sun (pages 12/13.)

His role as member of the Royal Academy of Fine Arts from 1780 onwards ensured gradual success. Eventually he was chosen to paint an altarpiece for the church of San Francisco el Grande in Madrid, which was finished in 1783 (pages 42/43). He wrote excitedly to his friend Zapater to tell him of his successes, his eyes always on the ultimate prize—to be court painter to Charles III who was a remote figure to Goya at this time despite an important commission to paint the First Minister Floridablanca in 1783 when Goya became official painter of the Spanish aristocracy. However, through Floridablanca, Goya was noticed by the king's recalcitrant brother, Don Luis de Borbón. It seems that through him the channels were open for success, with the young Goya spotting opportunities, playing them discretely and gaining himself a reputation for trustworthiness, which must have been essential at a time when the least misdemeanour could mean being in trouble with the all-powerful Inquisition.

It is interesting to note that even at this early stage in his career, Goya gives an insight into his ambitions and aspirations by including himself in key early commissions such as the altarpiece and *The Count of Floridablanca*. Through Floridablanca and Don Luis, Goya would meet and paint the young María Teresa de Borbón y Vallabriga, later the Countess of Chinchón (opposite).

It is unsurprising that Goya's journey continued with some of the great families of Madrid such as the Duke and Duchess of Osuna, who were members of the enlightened Spanish aristocracy (pages 50/51). One wonders what kind of conversations Goya had with his noble sitters and how he managed to marry his love of the ordinary street people of Madrid with his presence in elite circles who followed politics, fashions, literature and thought, all filtering to Spain from France. Perhaps a difficult balancing act! Certainly, his own predilection for and expertise in bird shooting offered him social status, with some esteeming him for this more than for his art.

By 1786 Charles III gave him a full-time salaried position as court painter to the king. The death of Charles III two years later, aged 72, in the early hours on 14 December 1788, and the coronation of Charles IV on 29 April 1789, with the French Revolution looming large, saw Goya, as First Court Painter to the new king, painting the Spanish royal family and the court in all its finery, aware perhaps of the precariousness of its position. The French Revolution presented a difficult situation for the king and the Spanish enlightened aristocracy. Charles IV was worried not only for his cousin Louis XIV's position as king but also for the potential spread of revolutionary ideas to Spain. He reached out numerous times to the French court despite the Inquisition's attempts to limit contact. Goya's thoughts about the French Revolution and its impact on the Spanish royal family as well as on laypeople are hard to assess. His letters give very little away about his interest in enlightened ideas, his approach to the church or how he felt about the royal family. He was clearly relieved to have work which allowed him to take care of his family and was excited by his own meteoric rise.

However, Goya fell ill for the first time in 1790, perhaps infected by his son Javier who had small-pox, leaving him in a weakened state. Smallpox was rife at the time and may account for the loss of several of Goya's children. By the end of 1792, Goya was forty-six, working hard and gradually gaining a reputation when he fell ill again. This time it was more serious. He was at the height of his career when he set off on a two month leave for Andalucía and suffered a collapse with 'colic'. He heard loud noises, fainted, had bouts of extreme dizziness and nausea and his balance was so badly affected, he could hardly stand up. In 1796 a treatise on lead poisoning listed similar symptoms and several artists were said to suffer from them. Indeed, we know from inventories listing Goya's supplies that he was using a lot of lead white. Goya never fully recovered, and the long-term result was acute deafness despite attempts at electrical healing.

Although Goya moved in high social circles, he was not well known amongst a broader public until 1815 when mention was made in a guidebook to Madrid. His appointment to Director of Painting at the San Fernando Royal Academy of Fine Arts in 1795 was a huge step forward both for his pocket and his reputation. It ensured a salary which meant he invested his savings and could indulge in the chocolate he loved, buy gold snuff boxes, take on a scribe, a new dog, more guns and even his own colour grinder.

However, he may have been rather isolated in his small circle at court, working in his studio on 1, Calle del Desengaño (Street of Disappointment) where he lived near the Puerta del Sol, suffering the loss of several of his own children and learning sign language. We begin to see him develop a more rebellious and satirical approach with im-agery of the hypocrisies of the church, witches and witchcraft and the horrors of the Inquisition. Goya spent much of the end of the eighteenth century caught on the one hand between his role of representing the stable monarchy and court as well as the demands of exalted clients, and on the other with his private work which so frequently

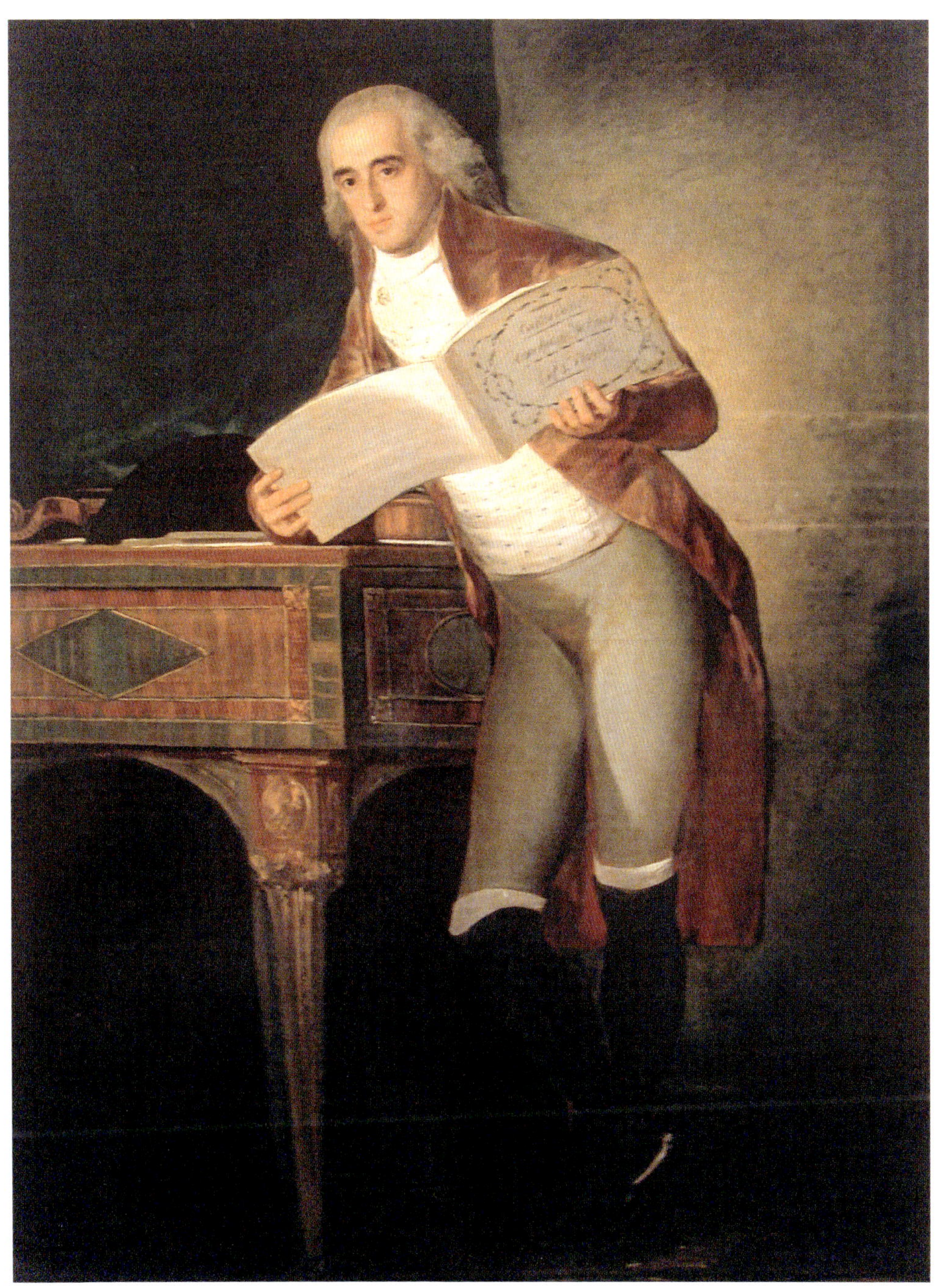

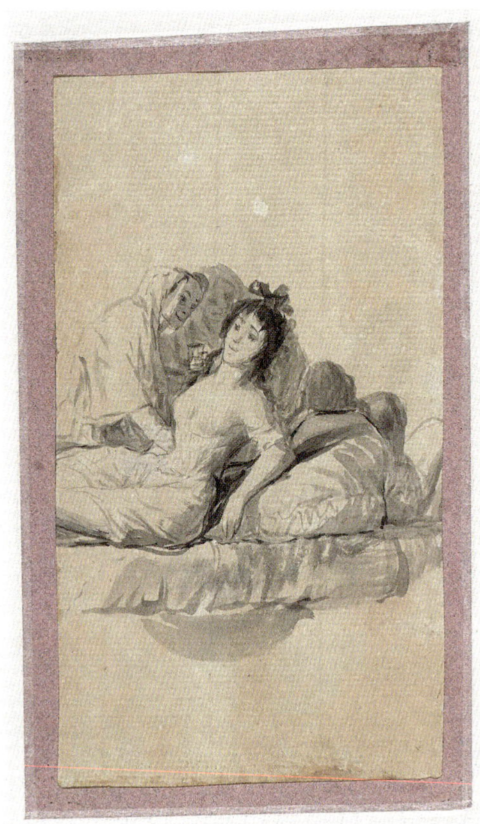

Two Young Women on a Bed (from the *Sanlúcar Album*), 1793-96

Duchess took Goya into her world, inviting him to her estate in Sanlúcar which he visited several times between 1796/97. He was fascinated by her and would continue to paint her face long after her death in 1802. In fact, her face became a template that he used in many of his sketches, etchings and paintings. The time he spent with her after the untimely death of her husband, provides valuable insights into many of Goya's facets: Goya the court painter and Goya the intimate describer of the everyday. The *Sanlúcar Album*, a private visual diary, includes a drawing of the Duchess holding her black adopted child Mar Luz—scandalous at the time—and there are also several sketches of semi-nude girls he met on the estate. These may have been the catalyst for *The Naked Maja* (pages 72/73) and we can also sense the influence of Velázquez's *Rokeby Venus* (c. 1650) which the Duchess owned.

The Duchess' affair with Manuel de Godoy, the Prime Minister, was as legendary as Queen María Luisa's, and the two women were great rivals. When Goya decided to paint a clothed *maja*, some ten years later (pages 20/21) we see a different palette and brushstroke. It has been suggested that *The Clothed Maja* was hung over the top of *The Naked Maja* with a pulley system so that the more revealing one could be peeped at underneath. A comparison between the two works suggests that in some ways although *The Naked Maja* was daring—especially at the time— and would lead to a conversation later with the Inquisition, *The Clothed Maja*, with her flimsy, figure-hugging dress which showed off her body,

began to address the ills of the society he knew so well. The conflict and his illness forced Goya to give up his academic teaching and towards the end of the century the artist was at a low ebb.

Just at this difficult time, the most beautiful woman, the Duchess of Alba, walked into his studio, demanding he paint her face. She was capricious, spoilt and married to the Duke of Alba (page 17) who was a refined, handsome gentle-man, known for his horse-riding skills and cultured character. The charismatic and high-ranking

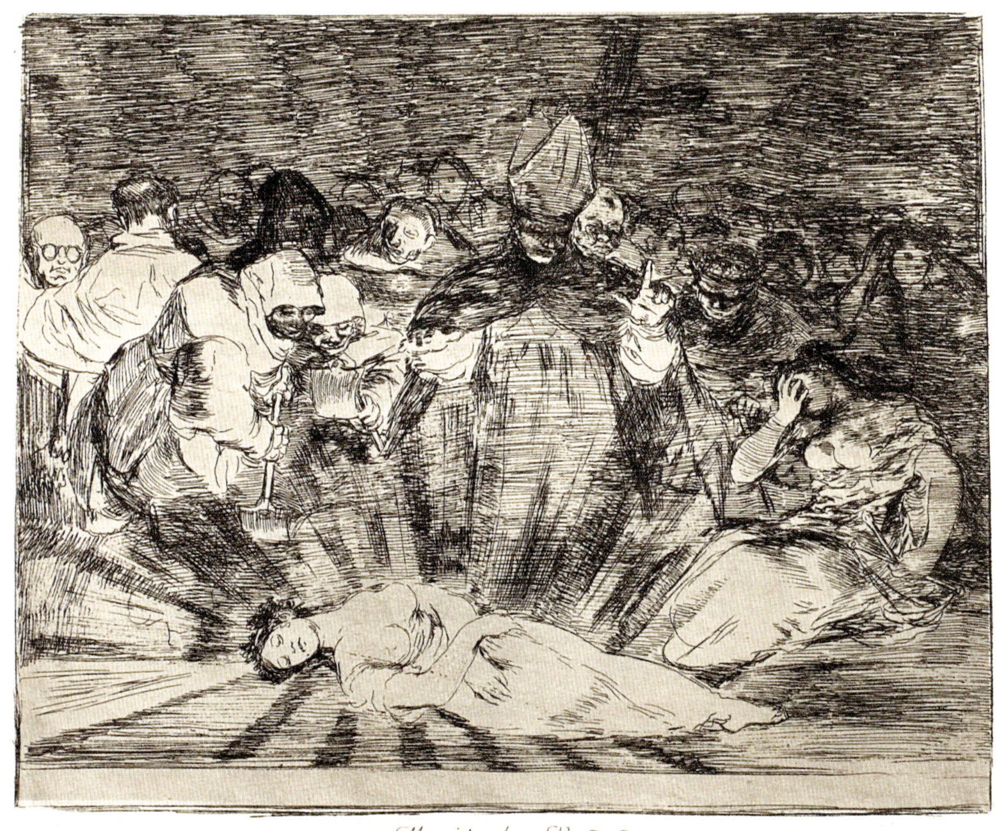

Truth Has Died, 1815–1820 (plate 79 from *The Disasters of War*)

coupled with her heightened blushing face, was perhaps even more sensual.

While Goya does not mention the Duchess of Alba in his writings, their relationship had a profound impact on him. In an etching which shows a woman certainly very similar to the duchess flying away like a witch without a broomstick, her tiny waist, black skirt, black mantilla and long dark hair along with the Latin title, *Volaverunt* (*They Have Flown*) (page 22) betrays a suggestion that whatever there had been between Goya and this extraordinary woman, it was now over and done with. The Duchess died of 'colic' under suspicious circumstances; it was said that she was influenced by witches and bullfighters. Even more bizarre was that the body was found with no feet when she was exhumed in 1945. Perhaps the coffin was too small, or the legends about this illustrious lady

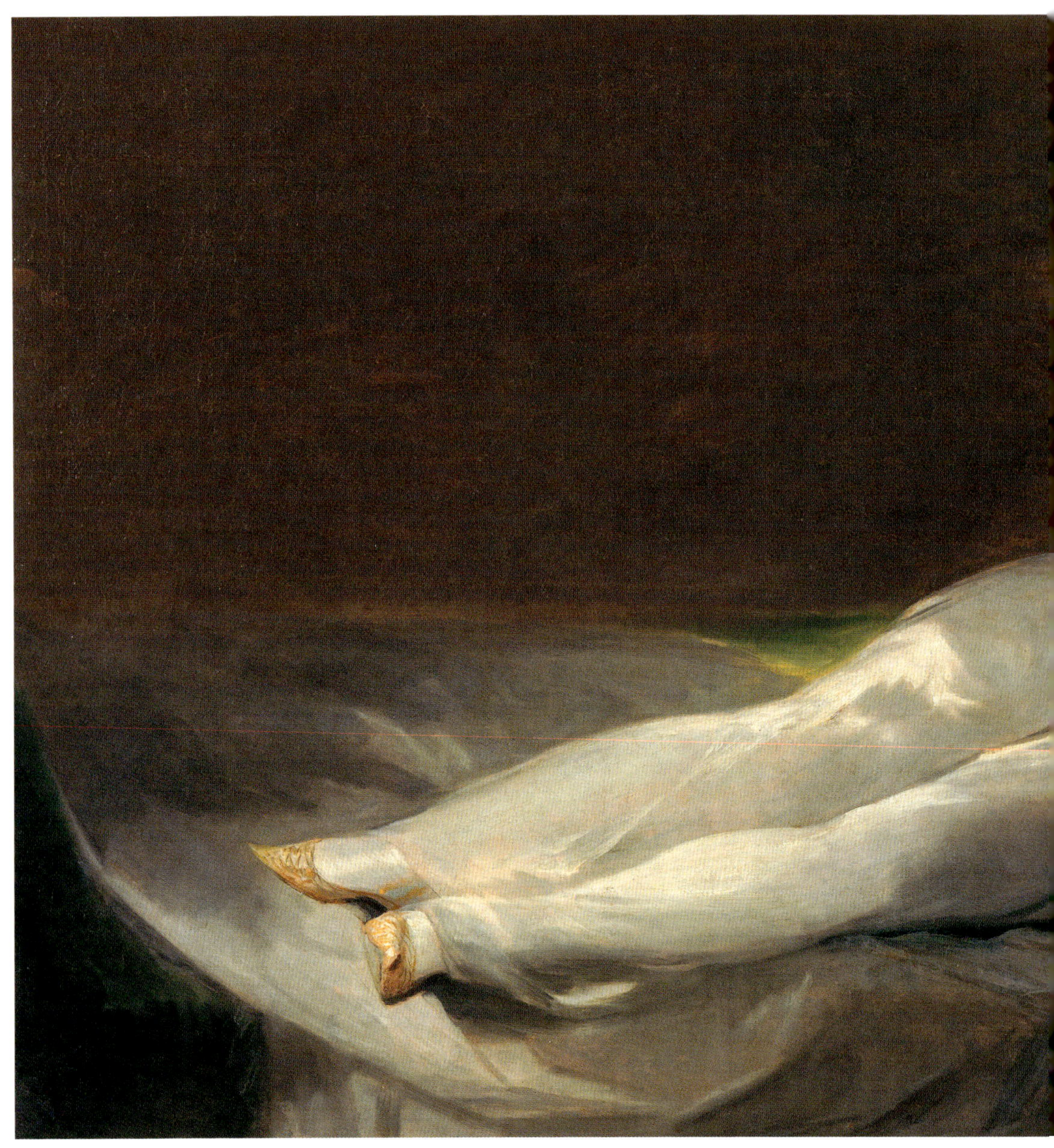

The Clothed Maja, c. 1805

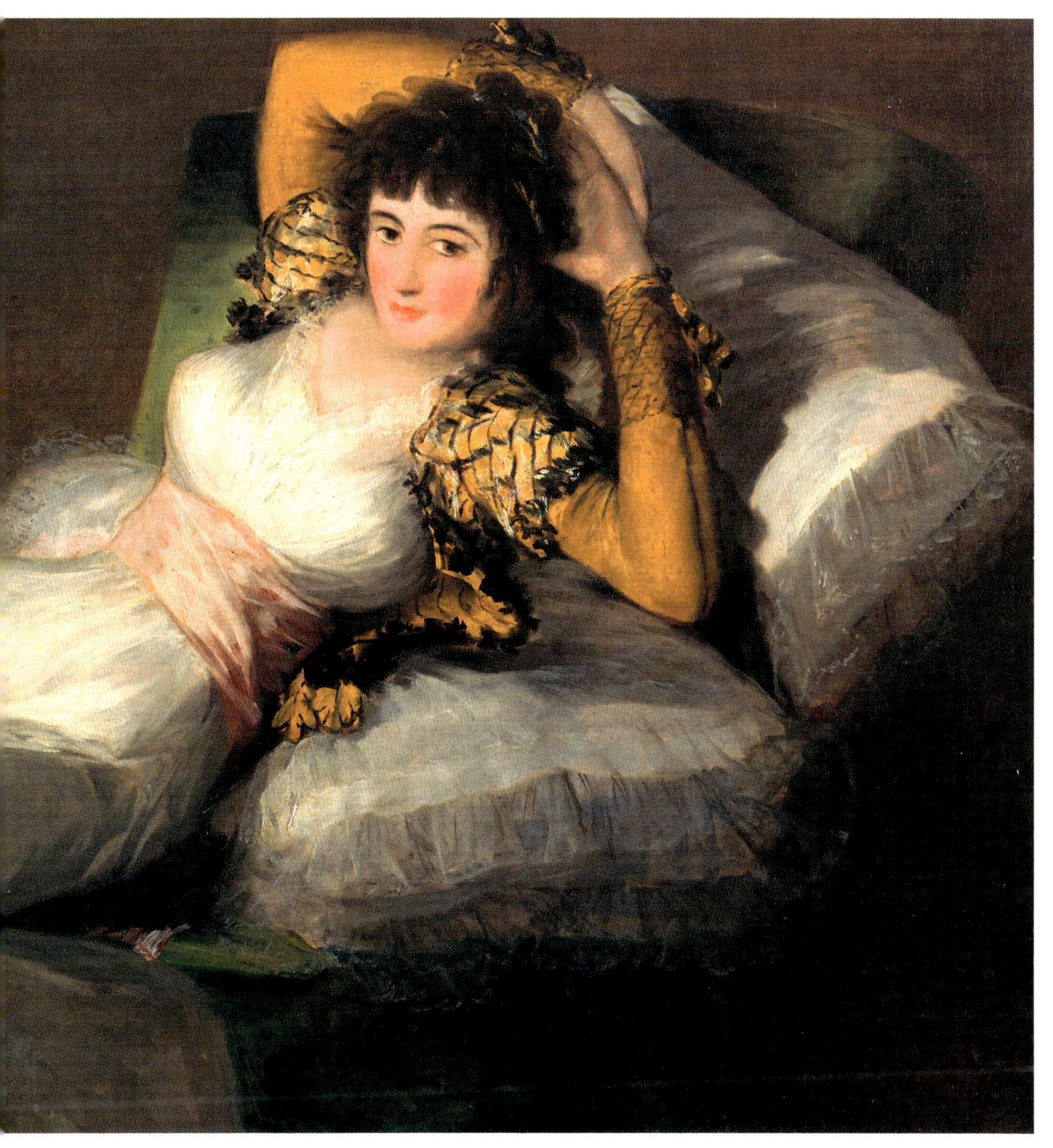

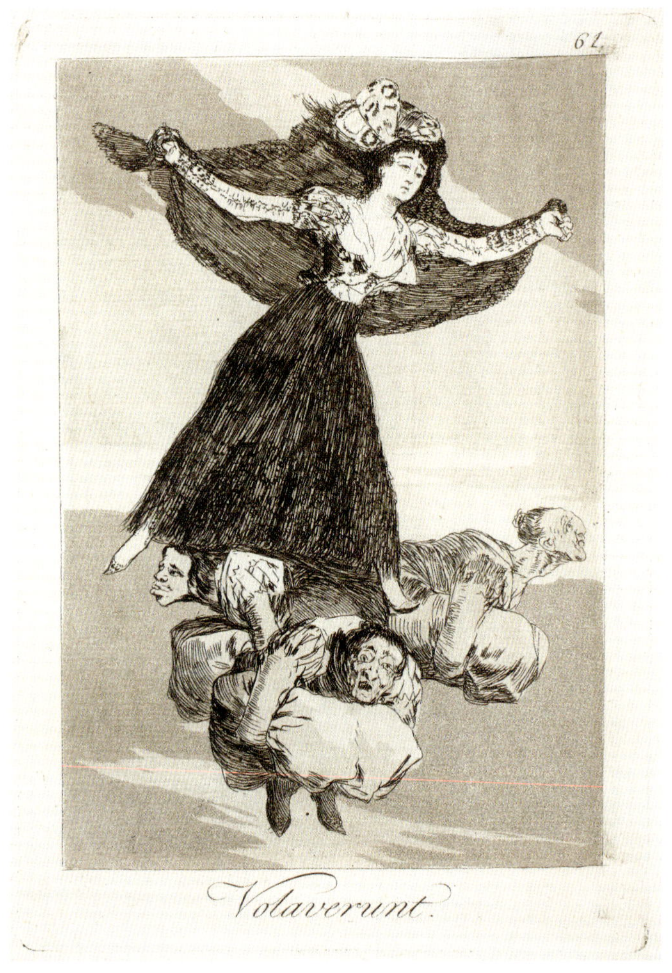

Volaverunt (*They Have Flown*), 1797/98

had tainted her reputation and someone took their revenge.

In 1798, while Goya painted frescoes of glorious female angels in the church of San Antonio de La Florida in Madrid—where he is now fittingly buried—he embarked on one of the most extraordinary periods of his career. The 1799 publication of *Los Caprichos*—a series of eighty aquatint etchings with brief explanations—was critical of superstition and social norms. They were quickly withdrawn from public sale although twenty-seven were sold. The etched plates were offered to Charles IV and the Royal Chalcography in 1803 in return for a pension for Goya's son Javier.

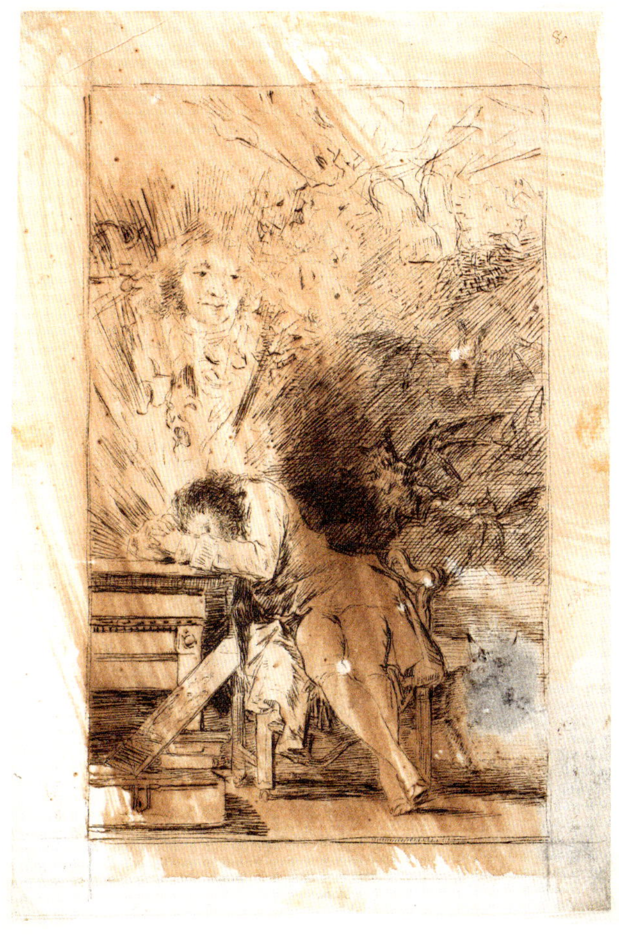

The Sleep of Reason Produces Monsters, 1797 (preparatory drawing)

The title *Los Caprichos* suggests a lightness of touch (caprice, whim) but these works are anything but light. In the early sketches for *The Sleep of Reason Produces Monsters* (above), a clue to Goya's approach to this body of work can be found. He watches his own sleep, willing himself to wake up and see life around him. In a slightly later version, he writes, "The author dreaming. His only purpose is to banish harmful ideas commonly believed and to perpetuate with this work of *Caprichos* the solid testimony of truth". *Truth Has Died* he will comment on another *Capricho* (page 19). Truth is his alibi for what is biting satire, but Goya is guarded. If he is targeting real people, they are so heavily disguised as to be unrecognisable. Is that the face of the Duchess of Alba (page 19)? We cannot be sure. Is that the unctuous Godoy? (pages 84/85). Again, there is no proof. A goat-footed satyr, lecherous old men, scheming young women, old crones pimping out younger women to men blinded by desire, gluttonous clergy, donkeys and witches, they all appear to perform the charade that is a portrait of life in Spain's capital.

Although Goya painted several of the Spanish *ilustrados* such as Gaspar Melchor Jovellanos, Meléndez Valdés and Leandro Fernandez Moratín, it is unlikely that they would have had long intellectual conversations with a mere painter, although the latter was a friend. However, their enlightened ideas would have filtered down to him and made him question the repression of intellectual freedom. In *Los Caprichos* Goya was careful to dissimulate, exploring betrothal as prostitution, ignorant beliefs and the church, brutality, the Inquisition, the backwardness of Spanish education and medical practices. It is surprising they were not banned, perhaps due to their prompt withdrawal or because the Inquisition, still a vehicle for terror, was focussing less on enforcing Catholic beliefs and more on ensuring state security. No one avoids Goya's wrath, however, in his more private works: the idle rich and ignorant poor; those who ban bullfighting as a sop to enlightened thinking; and the donkeys that are blind, lazy followers.

The dawn of a new century saw few changes. Goya's role was now First Painter to the King, with a salary of 50,000 reales and a luxurious carriage. But the next few years would see the rise of Napoleon in France and the fall of the House of Bourbon. Goya's brief was to show that the Bourbon court was strong and united, wealthy in its costumes and ruled by good humane monarchs. His full-length and his equestrian portraits of the monarchs do exactly that. The queen (opposite) is dressed in full Spanish costume with mantilla and fan. It is unknown if there were any sumptuary laws in Spain at this time, as her tiny silk shoes have threaded gold and her mantilla with its dainty pink ribbon were made from the finest lace from Brussels. Time and pregnancies (twenty-four of them) took their toll on the queen, but Goya did his level best, wrapping her up in black lace like a dainty morsel. The king (page 26) is relaxed and portrayed in full hunting gear with no care in the world but to grasp a large gun and be adored by his dog. If Goya thought the king was indolent or apathetic we do not know, but the presence of medals, sash, shorts and tights suggests a humorous take. The equestrian portraits, inviting comparison with Velázquez, exude notions of power, nobility, strong leadership and control. Goya does his best to present a viable royal family, approachable and benevolent.

The artist's professional standing was very dependent on patronage from the king, queen and the all-powerful Godoy. Prime Minister Godoy, known in Spain as *el choricero* (the sausage maker) because his father was a butcher, was much maligned by the envious who saw him as a coward, hiding behind the queen's skirts, disparaging

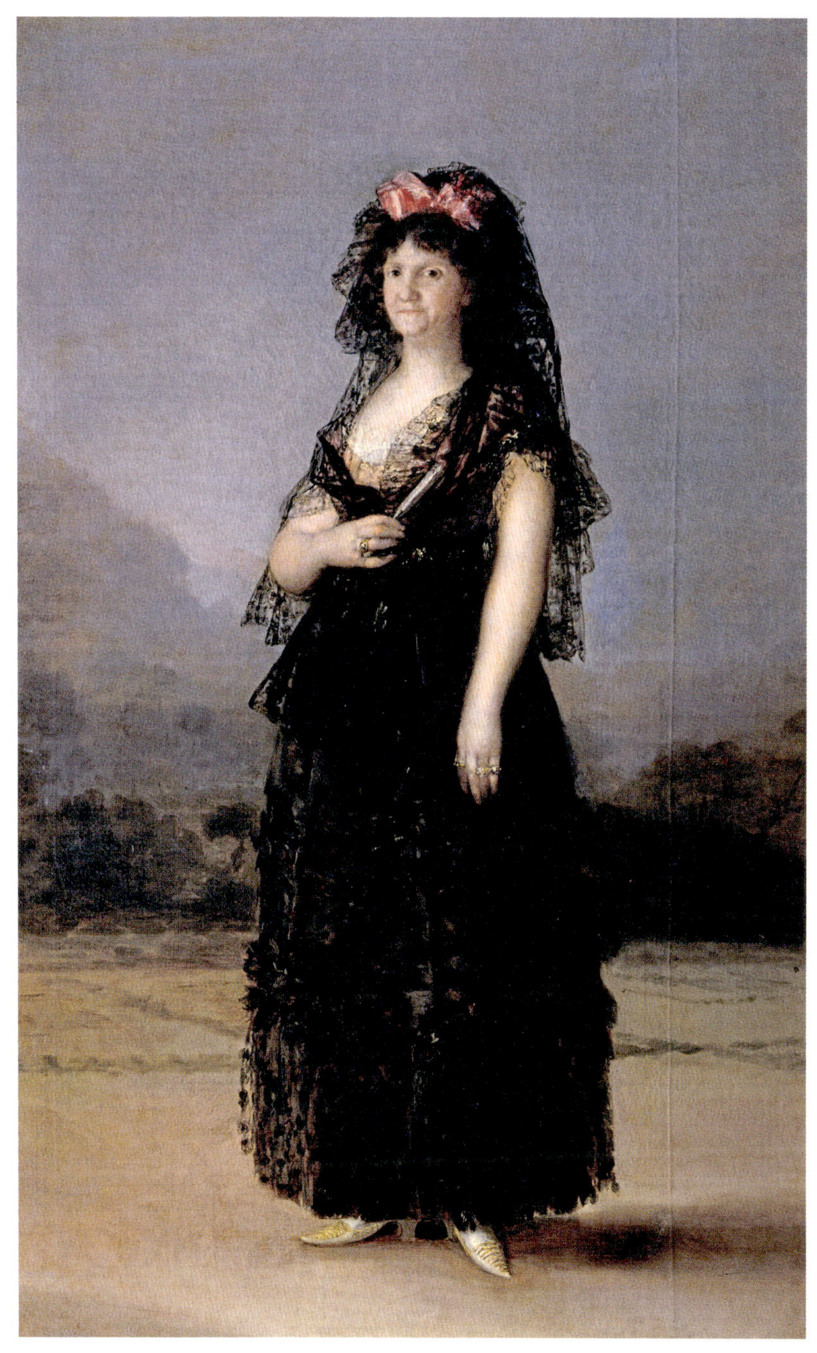

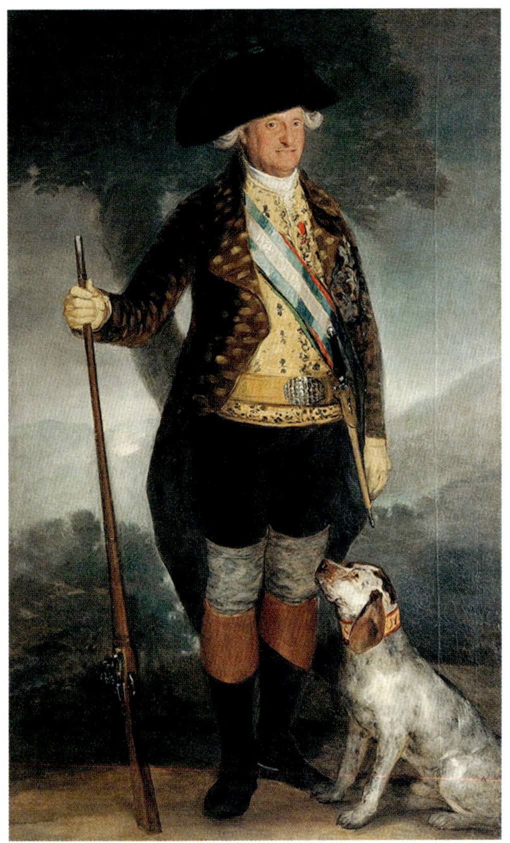

Charles IV in Hunting Dress, 1799

of his wife, the Countess of Chinchón, and in love, as everyone was, with the Duchess of Alba. Overconfident and arrogant but hard-working, Godoy was given the title of Prince of Peace in 1795 after he negotiated the Treaty of Basel which ended the War of the Pyrenees between Spain and Revolutionary France. Godoy's navy was defeated by Britain in Trafalgar in 1805 and his subsequent hair-brained scheme to invade Portugal and repel the British in partnership with Napoleon—documented in a treaty signed by Charles IV at Fontainebleau—was a failure. While the Spanish army never reached the Algarve as planned, Napoleon's army did cross into Spain making it vulnerable to Napoleon's ambitions and sparking the Peninsular War known as the War of Independence. Godoy went into exile in France with Charles IV and María Luisa and their son, the Prince of Asturias.

With war raging and Napoleon's brother Joseph ruling Spain, Goya's activities as court painter had withered, but he documented the terrible conflict with some extraordinary works capturing death and decay such as *Still Life of Sheep's Ribs and Head (A Butcher's Counter)* (c. 1808–12, pages 86/87). Dead birds and fish are strewn across the canvas. His *Still Life with Golden Bream* (1808–12, pages 28/29), was set on a moonlit shore where we might imagine soldiers disembarking. The dead fish, piled high like human bodies, are rheumy and wide eyed as if we are witnessing their very dying moment; and the transition from life to death is caught in gleaming orange tones. Goya portrays the bloodiness and price of war which he will live and breathe for six long years.

During that time Goya must have felt isolated and alone. He would have felt the loss of his childhood friend and confident Martín Zapater who died in 1803 (page 30); and he was unmoored from his exiled royal patrons and other enlightened clientèle. He also lost his wife Josefa in 1812 during the famine in Madrid. His salary was stopped for a while when he was under investigation, along with many others, for his political conduct during the period leading up to the French invasion. Proving

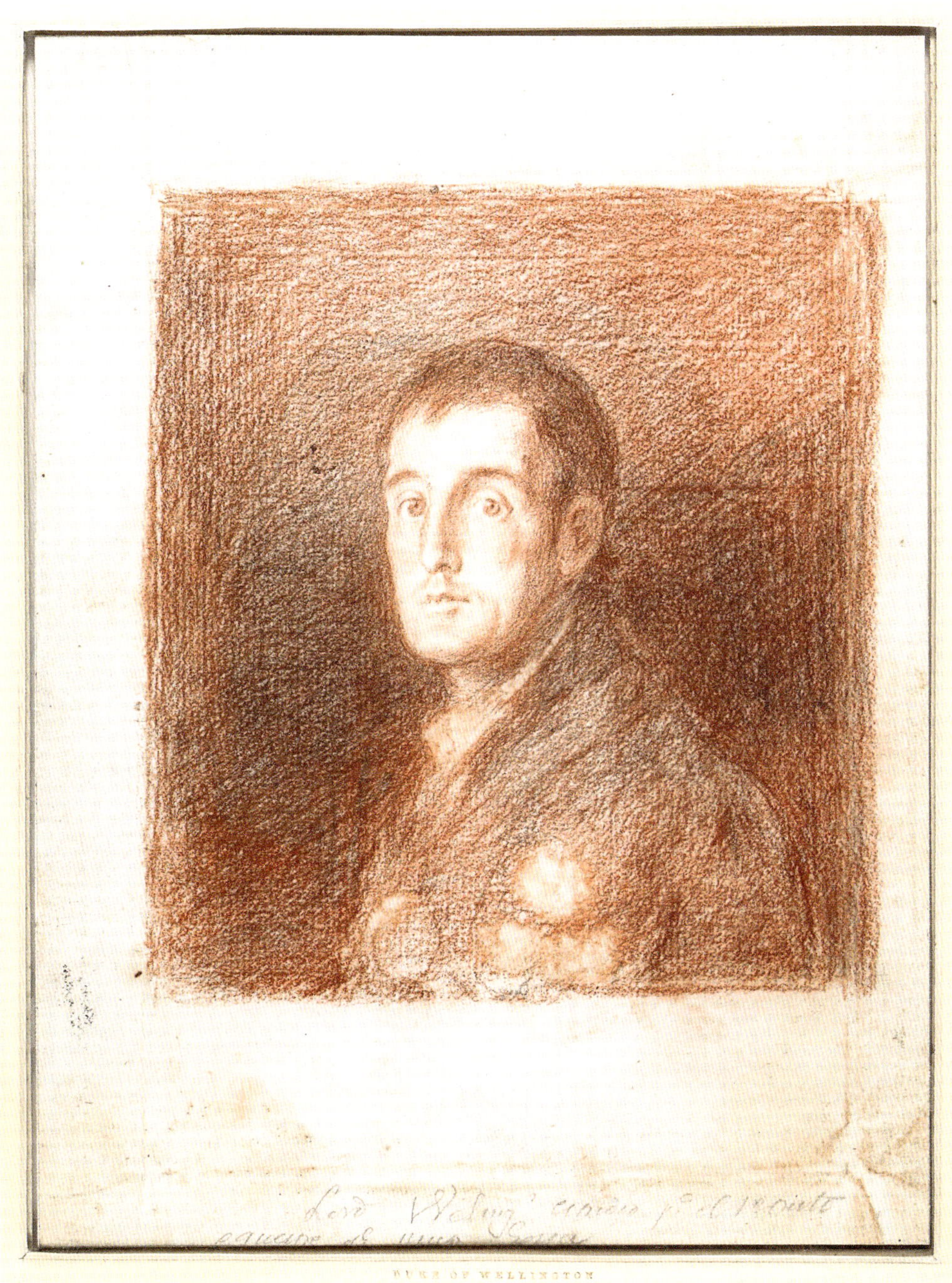

DUKE OF WELLINGTON

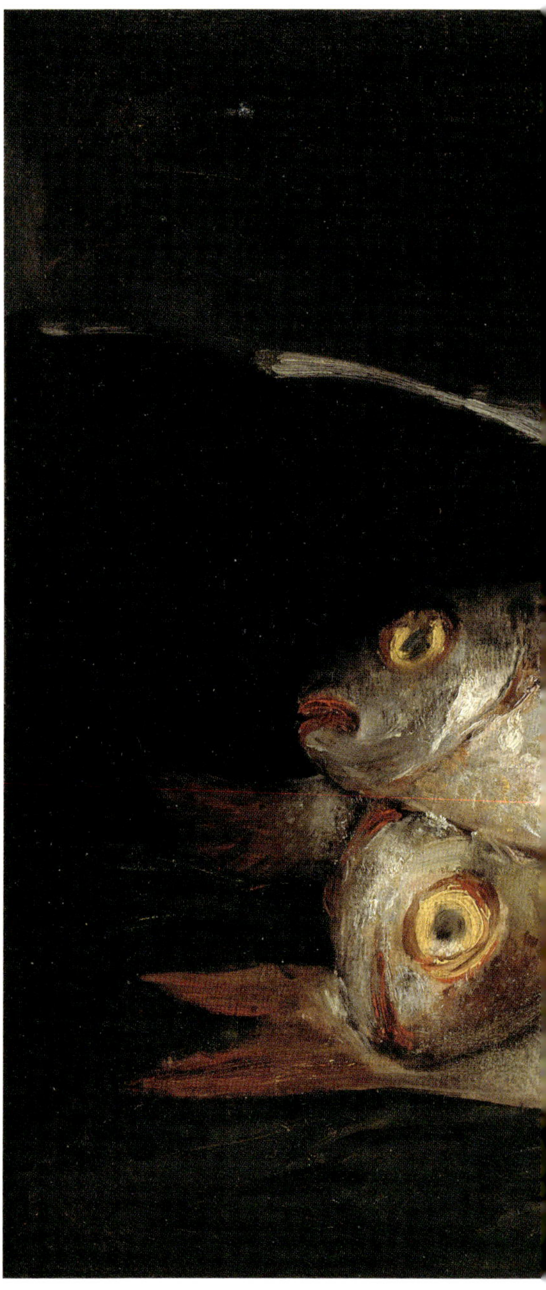

his resilience Goya became a war artist in his sixties. His actual commissions were not numerous but behind the scenes he reveals much about the effect of war on the people. Two works stand out. The critical events events of 3 May (pages 94/95) would only be painted after the war was over in 1814. Its companion piece depicting the events of 2 May were commissioned by King Ferdinand VII to commemorate the overthrow of the tyrannical Napoleon (pages 32/33). Two Spanish heroes, Velarde and Daoiz, who gave arms to insurgents against the explicit command of Napoleon, were killed and Goya chose an incident in the Puerta del Sol of the mob revolting against the Marmelukes, who were fighting for the French. Goya presents us once again with a fabulous contrast between ordinary people, muleteers, shoemakers, bakers and others against the French Cuirassiers who were *moros* or dark-skinned. This is a stark reminder, of course, of the 800 years Spain was under Islamic rule. As they tussle wildly, body against body, flesh against flesh, trampled underfoot in the swirling reds and yellows of the scene, the ordinary Spaniards' intense struggle is captured by Goya as they revolt against a foreign tyrant.

Throughout the war years and beyond Goya returned to the medium of etching to expose the violence of battle and its effect on everyday people. Not published until thirty-five years after his death, Goya called them *Fatal Consequences of Spain's Bloody War with Bonaparte, and Other Emphatic Caprices*, including the word *Capricho* he had used a decade previously. In all there are eighty-five prints in this series—also known as

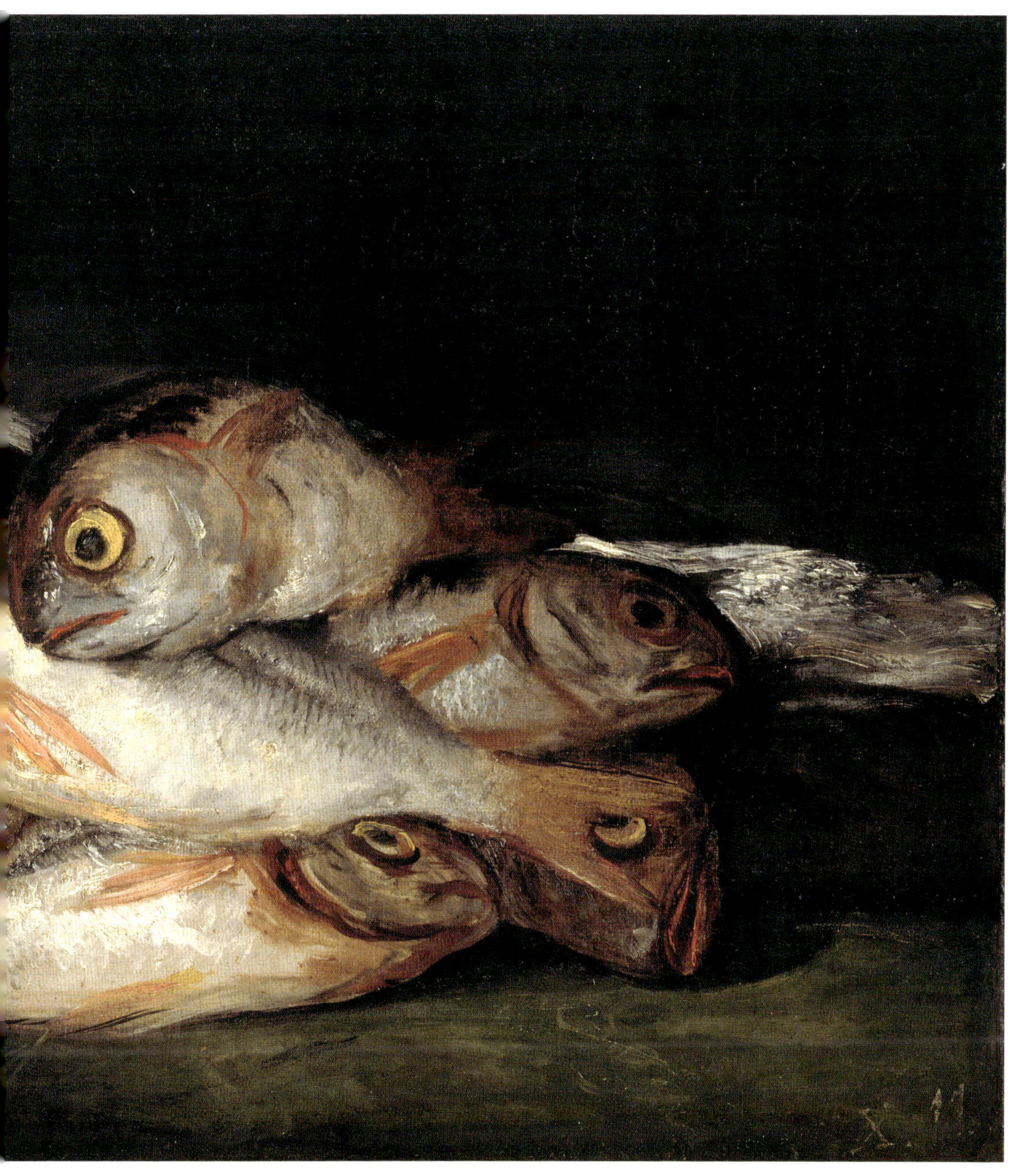

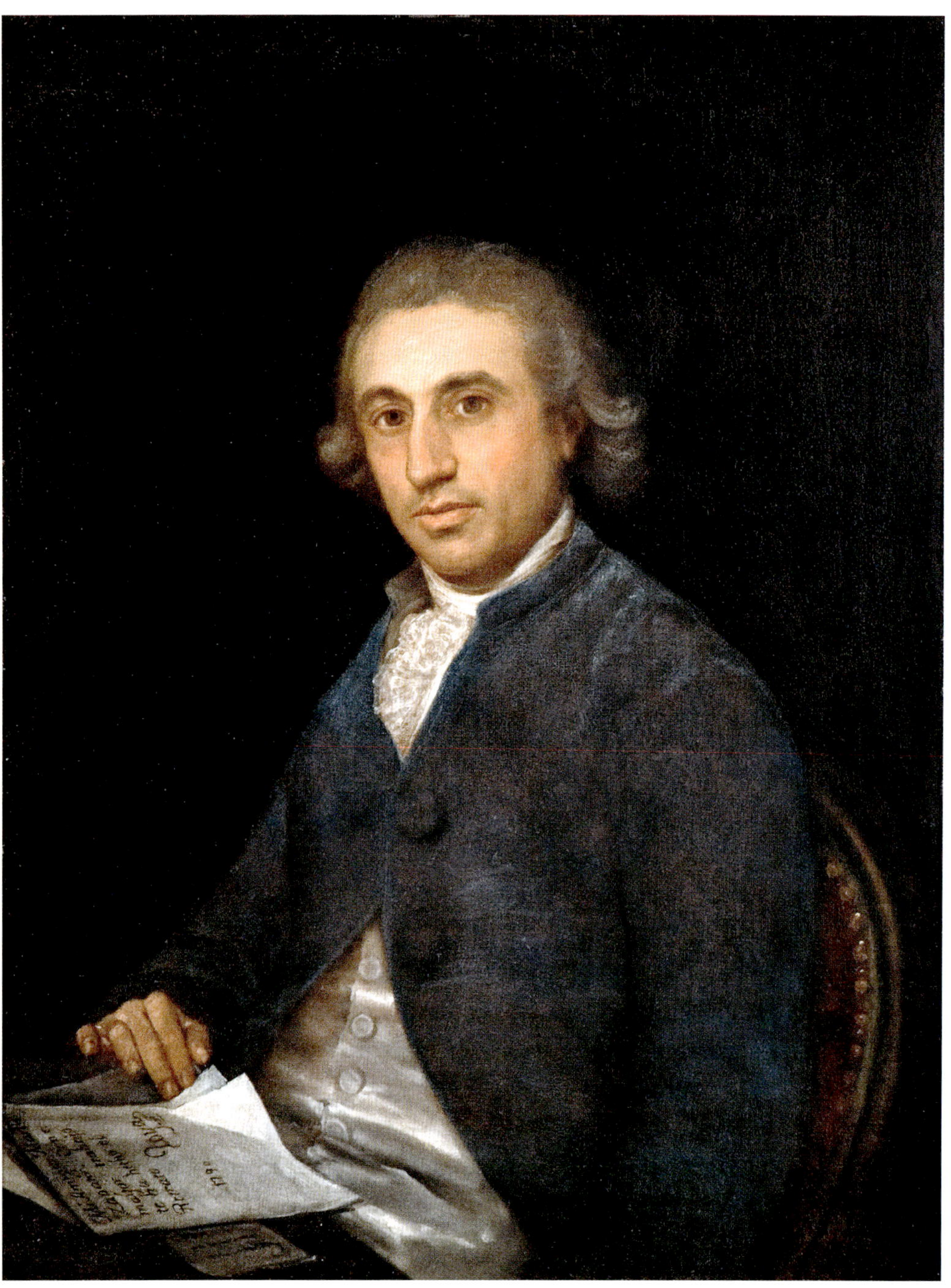

The Disasters of War— divided into three groups. The first group of forty-seven deals with the effect of war on civilians and soldiers; the second group looks at the famine in Madrid, a particularly poignant moment for Goya; and the last group analyses the disappointment of liberal-minded Spaniards with the rejection of the Constitution of 1812 by the restored Bourbon monarchy under Ferdinand VII and the church.

This Constitution of 1812, seen to be one of the most liberal of all times, affirmed national sovereignty, the separation of powers and the freedom of the press. It encouraged free enterprise, government sponsorship of primary education and suffrage for men over twenty-five. It aimed to abolished torture and corporate privileges and established a constitutional monarchy with a parliamentary system. It also upheld Catholicism as the sole legal religion in Spain. It is argued that if the Constitution had been accepted, Spain would not have suffered a civil war in the twentieth century.

As *The Disasters of War* dealt with the effects of war in stark black and white they deny us all beauty. Beauty dies with war. The Peninsular War put a stop to all the street gossip. The bald facts of a gruesome period of Spanish history are powerfully laid bare in these timeless works which we are left to put into the context of our own existences. The political backdrop and the terrible sights Goya claimed to have seen first-hand during these vicious wars, provide a different image of women and men; capricious witches, incarcerated victims, ruthless heroines, women struggling to stay alive;

men dismembered and dying, and those who do the killing are brutal in their destruction. Goya's world view was indeed darkened by famine, cruelty, poverty and the denial of a new enlightened country under King Ferdinand VII. The stark realism records the tumultuous history of his era and the demise of the old regime. We see the power of horror and these etchings make uncomfortable viewing; mutilated torsos, bodies hung from trees, the torture, rape and disintegration of especially female bodies, starving, cradling dead sons and wielding bayonets.

By 1814 *Truth Has Died* (page 19). Through the lens of Goya's women once more we see his cynical dissent, his loneliness and his decision that truth has indeed died. "Yo lo vi" (I saw it), Goya writes and as a witness to such horrors he expanded his notion of Woman as the incarnation of Beauty to include courage and fearlessness. Augustina of Aragon, during the siege of Zaragoza, fired a twenty-four-pounder cannon and became famous for her bravery (pages 90/91). Women rarely fought in the war but spent most of their time protecting their children or their own integrity. But Augustina rose to the occasion, murderous, she took revenge on those who profited from war and defiled her sisters. In the raw images of rape and brutality, Goya forces the viewer to confront the horror. One of the added etchings called *Emphatic Caprice*, which refers to the authoritarian restoration of Ferdinand VII and Goya's eventual decision to leave court, claims "Truth Has Died and Will She Rise Again?" in the form of a woman lying dead on the ground surrounded by the staring faces of disbelief of those who try to bury her. The jagged scratching of the marks echoes the juddering creative act, almost too painful to display. Goya had no audience for these works, they resemble a visual diary, a record of events not for posterity but to exorcise his own horror.

The war would end, in no small part thanks to the success of the Duke of Wellington in defeating the French invaders. Hailed as a Spanish Grandee in 1814—this red chalk over black chalk and graphite drawing on paper has an extraordinary intensity—Lord "Weling" (on inscription) looks as though he has just come off the battlefield (page 27). The exhausted duke, weakened from battle, wide-eyed and drawn, is not displayed as a conquering hero despite his military success. The accompanying note from Mariano, Goya's grandson, mentions that the drawing was hidden amongst other prints. He also suggests that it was executed in Alba de Torres, after the Battle of Arapiles near Salamanca (22 July 1812) but it is difficult to imagine that the then sixty-six-year-old Goya would have been at the front. It was drawn more likely back in Madrid where the duke had arrived on 12 August. This drawing is probably a preparatory work for an equestrian portrait of him as well as a half-length portrait (pages 92/93). It was also possibly intended to be used as a print which we can see from the platemark. On the back is a study in black chalk of Fray Juan Fernández de Rojas—an historian, writer and humourist of the School of Salamanca.

In 1814 when Goya asked Ferdinand VII if he could paint the most notable and heroic actions and scenes of the glorious insurrection against the tyrant of Europe, he proved that there was still fight in him

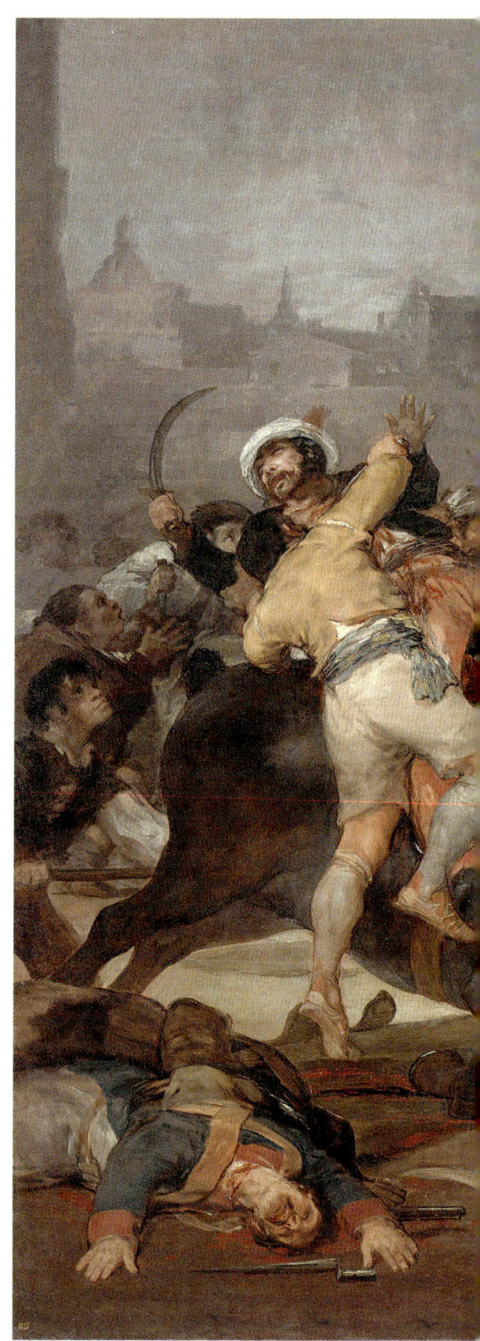

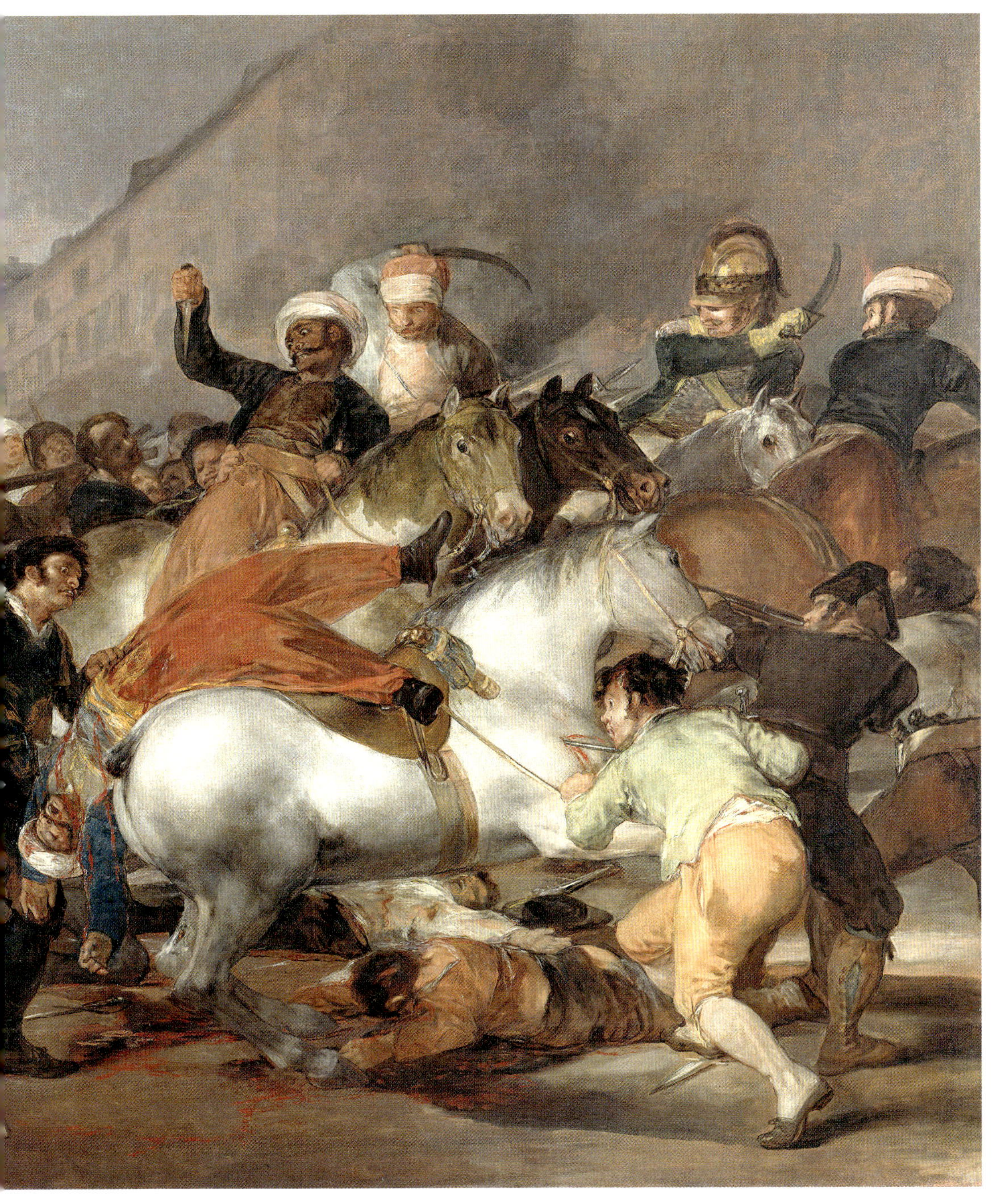

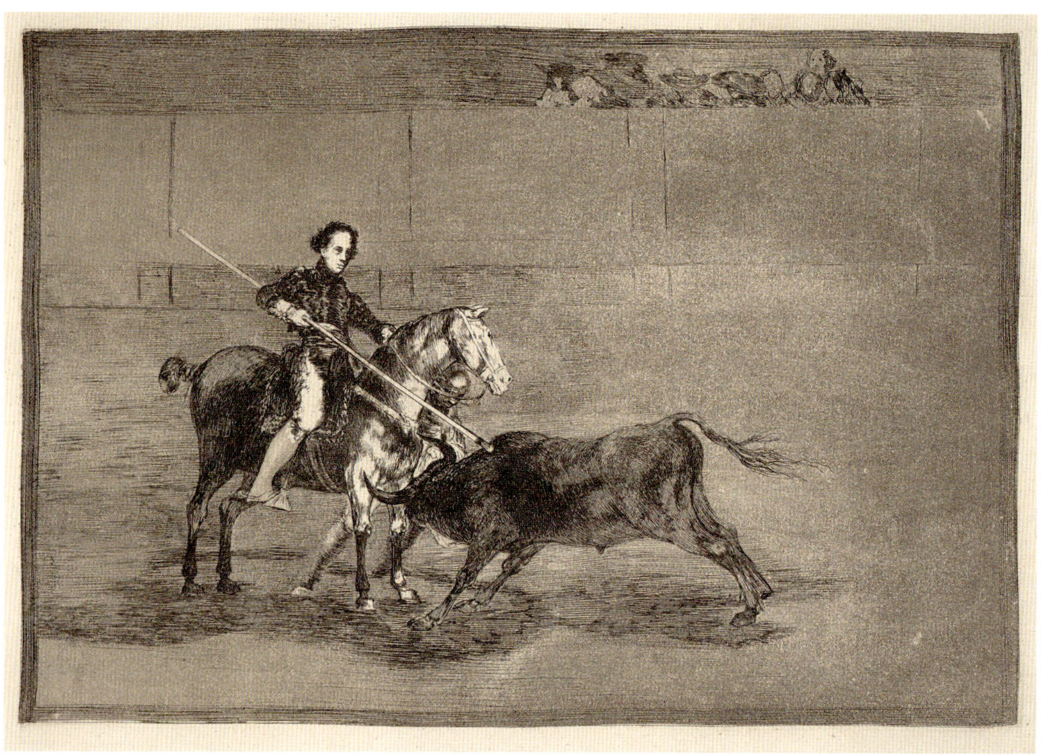

Manly courage of the notorious Pajuelera [in the bull ring] at Zaragoza, 1814-16 (plate 22 of The Art of Bullfighting*)*

yet. He was also to, possibly unwillingly, paint a portrait of a king he clearly despised (pages 96/97) and from whom he had to beg frequently for payment. So, what did a future at court hold for Goya?

We have seen the painter looking into the mirror as he gradually aged. The self-portrait of 1815 (pages 100/101) is evidence of a life filled with turmoil. He has witnessed the death of six children, he has seen the French invasion of Spain, answered to the Inquisition, lost his wife and dealt with one too many king. On the inscription he proudly included his roots in Aragon. Perhaps looking back

at his youth as a country kid in Zaragoza playing at bullfights, Goya embarked on yet another series, the *Tauromachia (The Art of Bullfighting)* which was completed roughly between 1814–1816. When compared with *The Disasters of War* it is easy to see parallel violence, but this series also has a hint of homage and nostalgia. With this history of bullfighting and of Spain itself, Goya takes the viewer back to the time of Muslim Spain, via noble sport within royal circles and on to his own time when bullfighters were friends and part of his childhood, referring frequently to well-known and loved fighters, female and male, such as Nicolosa

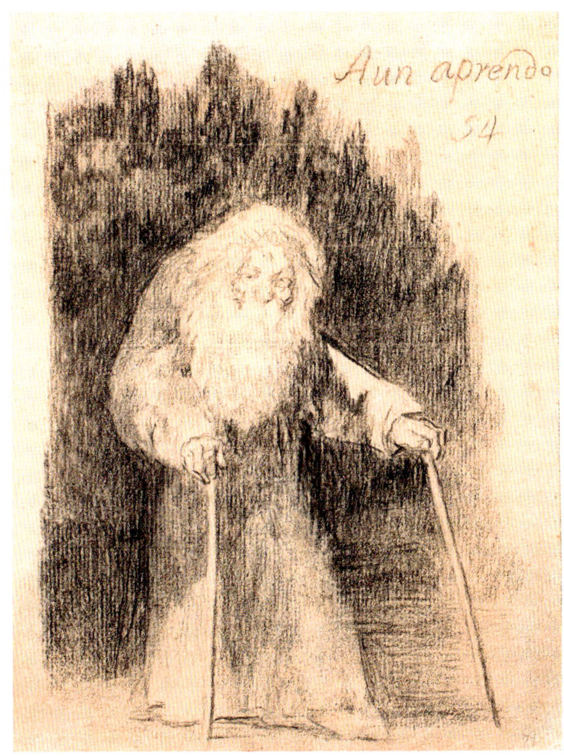

Aún Aprendo, 1824–28

Escamilla, known as La Pajuelera (opposite), a match seller by day, and of course Pedro Romero. Goya claimed to have fought bulls and indeed in the self-portrait done in the studio he portrays his bullfighting jacket (pages 60/61).

But this is all a prelude to Goya's escape from court and from the terrible reign of Ferdinand VII.

On 27 February 1812, Goya had bought a run-down house with twenty-three acres of arable land for 60,000 reales. At last, he was a gentleman landowner. The previous proprietors may have had the two floors of walls painted with pleasant scenes which possibly prompted Goya to cover them up, every single one. He moved in on 17 February 1819, with his housekeeper and probably mistress, Leocadia Weiss, but illness struck again that year. Goya seems to have been unsure whether he would live and was certainly grateful when doctor Arrieta (pages 106/107) pulled him back from death's door. Who knows when he began covering the walls in oil paint to create what are now known as the *Black Paintings*? Did he ever intend anyone to see these outpourings or were they simply an old man's visually incoherent set of private ramblings? Were they testimony to his freedom from court or pure despair? Leocadia appears along with yokels fighting, the gods cutting the umbilic cord of the earth, Saturn devouring his son, pilgrims, goats, old crones, a dog barking, witches and Fates—a veritable panoply of humanity. One might say that many of the characters had been part of Goya's repertoire but here he smothered and lathered them onto barely sized walls, daubing and scraping, pouring and wiping. The artist appeared to be exorcising the horror of the years before, a task that will have taxed him both mentally and physically. We do not know how long it took him or how it affected his health. These are monsters of the imagination, the children of Black Spain. They are not entirely black in colour—the word seems to relate more to the subject matter itself—and it is difficult to imagine what they must have looked like before they were hacked off the walls, restored by Martín Cubells, repainted where necessary and then rehung in 1874 at the Paris World Fair before they finally found their way to the Prado Museum.

Goya's conclusion was that he was still learning (page 35). We might think he was on the brink of death, a nervous breakdown or even insanity. None of it. He signed over the deeds of the house to his grandson in 1823 and pretended to be on a health mission to take the waters in Plombières in France. He made off across the border, as his king and queen had done before, to join other Spanish exiles. For the last few years of his life in Bordeaux he continued to work, drawing for the most part and taking up lithography. Ferdinand VII granted him a pension in 1826 for his long service to the Crown and Goya returned a couple of times to Madrid where he was painted by Vicente López Portaña (opposite). The artist's health declined upon his return to Bordeaux, and he died on 16 April 1828. Goya's remains were exhumed in 1901 and transferred to Madrid. In 1929 he was moved, without his skull, to the little church of San Antonio de La Florida where he lies under his own dome frescoes and glorious angels.

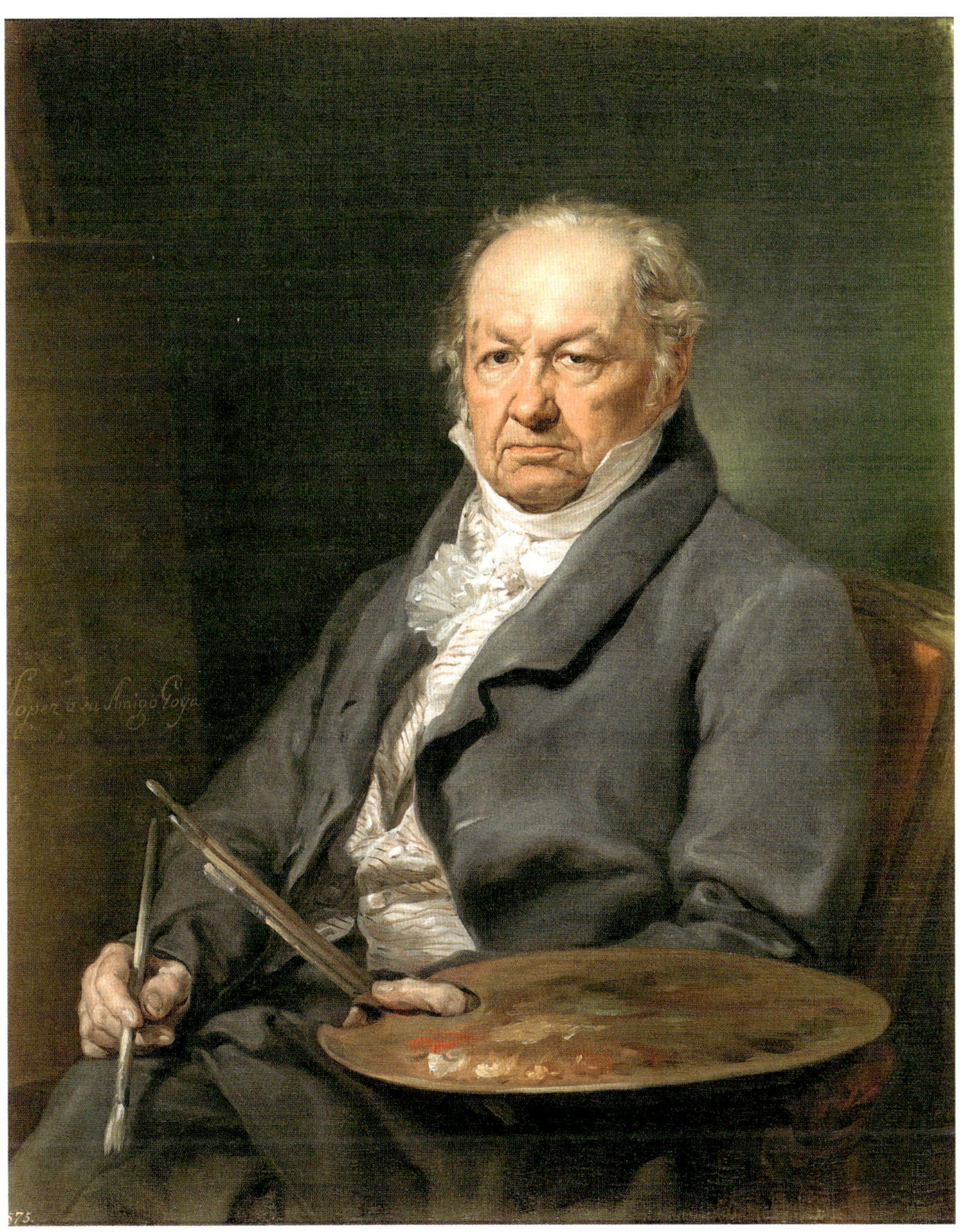

Vicente López Portaña, *The Painter Goya*, 1826

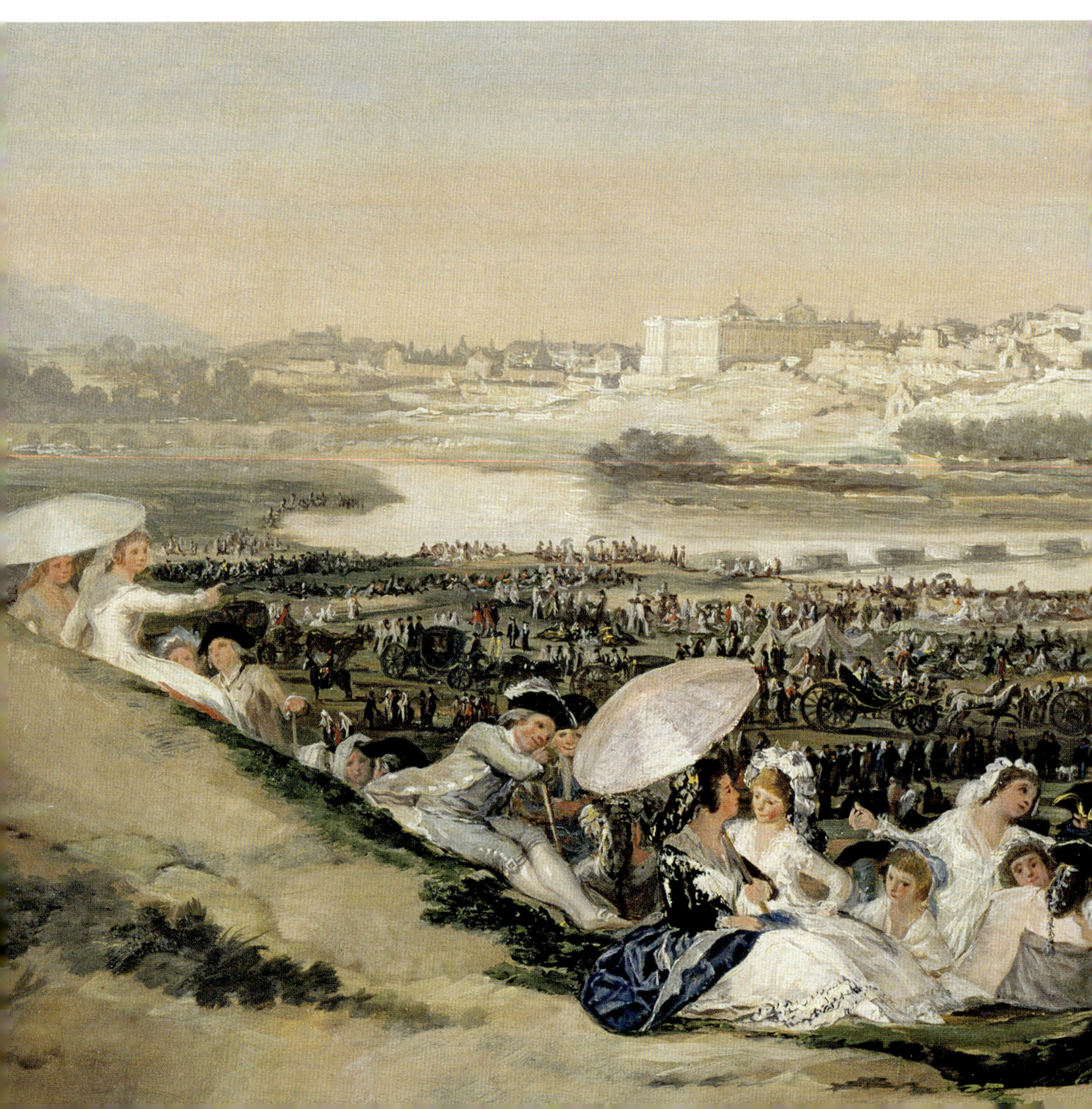

WORKS

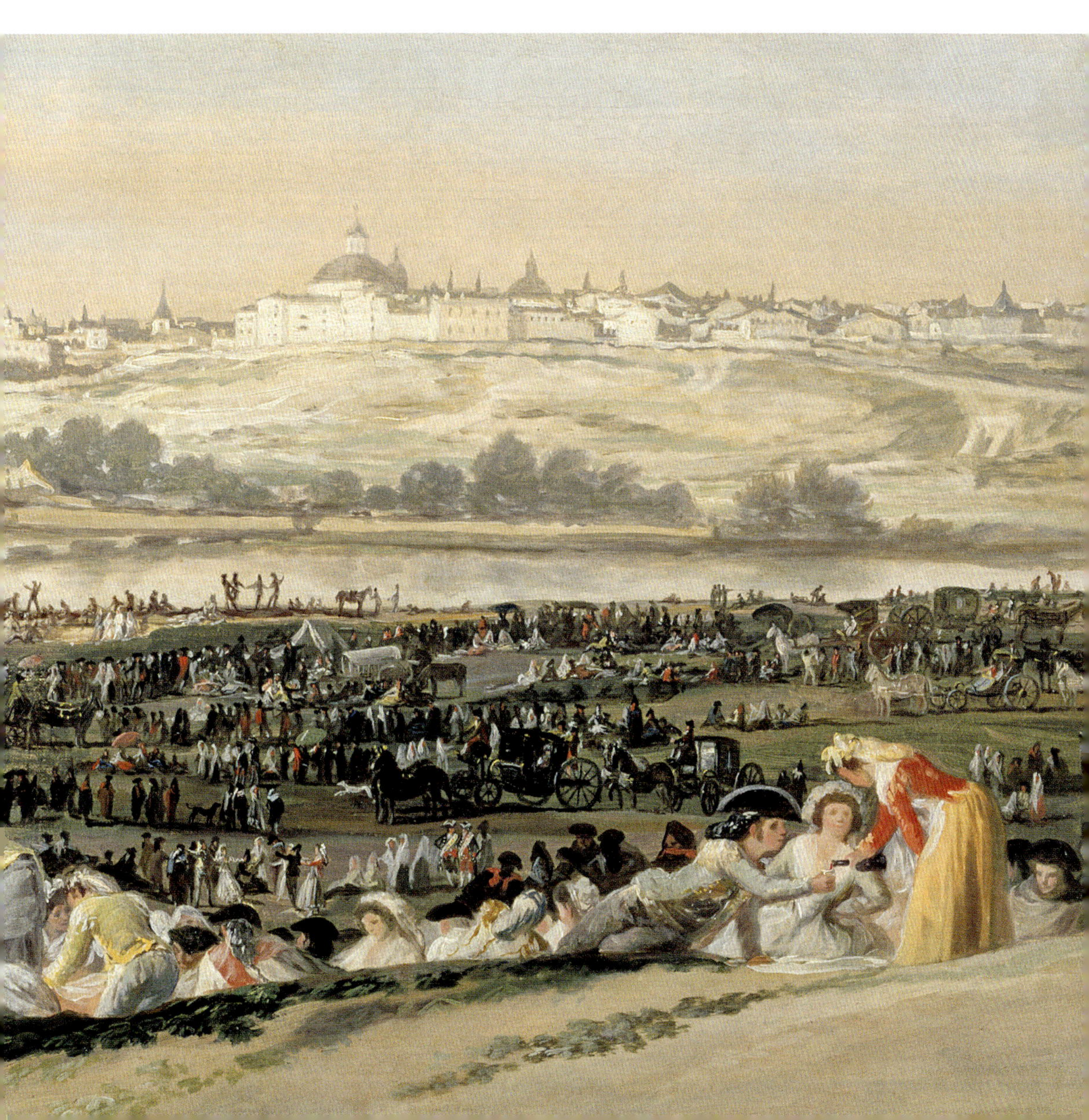

The Blind Guitarist (Tapestry Cartoon), 1778

Oil on canvas
260 x 311 cm
Museo del Prado, Madrid

This tapestry cartoon design was so big that it was initially rejected by the weavers
as apparently it had too many figures. Goya was asked to do corrections to facilitate
the transition from painting to tapestry. In his letters he described fourteen characters
including a "black waterseller". It may have been turned down due to the disturbing
eyeless face of the blind musician whose head is tilted backwards as he sings his
couplets; his half open mouth displays just a couple of teeth. Goya would have seen
blind musicians begging on the streets of Madrid, especially during the annual fair,
probably in the Plaza de la Cebada (Barley Square). The left-hand side shows a native
of Murcia pulling oxen. Goya's focus on eccentric outcasts or the less fortunate will be
evident throughout his career. The young prince of Asturias and his wife María Luisa,
who commissioned the tapestry to decorate the antechamber to their bedroom, were
interested in and relaxed about the uncomfortable quality of this kind of street theme.
Accustomed to *Commedia dell'arte* and Spanish *sainetes*—comic opera pieces using
scenes from street life—the young royals were more open in their tastes than many at
the time. This work is filled with certain character types; *majos*, (dandies), well dressed
figures, Murillo-like urchins reminiscent of Lazarillo, (that picaresque hero of literature,
published anonymously in 1554); they all mingle around the guitarist and his chubby
assistant. At the apex of the composition is a man on a horse. The couple in yellow seem
sympathetic to the plight of the musician and he looks for change in his pocket—the lady
clearly admires his gesture. Life in its many guises is portrayed here perhaps to remind
those who are wealthier of their good fortune.
By 1778, Goya's private life was overwhelmed by the loss of children, some of which
did not even come to term and only one, Javier, born later in 1784, would survive into
maturity. This must have been a heartbreaking time for Goya and for Josefa Bayeu, his
wife of five years. At the Royal Tapestry Factory of Santa Barbara where he worked,
he designed pieces for the royal palaces, choosing subjects which were alien to the
riches of court; frequently rural life with its street urchins, its festivals and all manners
of delights, very reminiscent of Tiepolo who had arrived at court in April 1762 and whom
Goya had probably seen in Italy previously in 1770 or 1771.

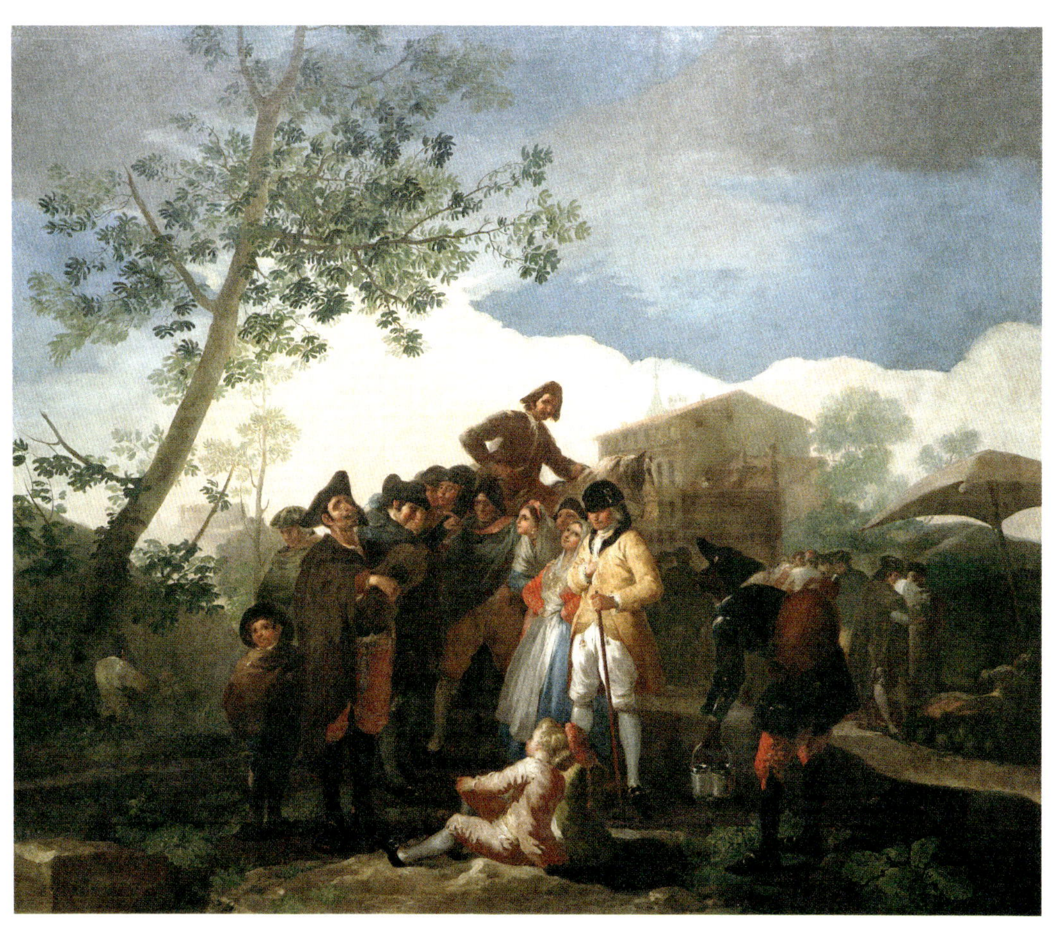

Saint Bernardino of Siena Preaching before Alfonso of Aragon, 1781–83

Oil on canvas
480 x 300 cm
Church of San Francisco El Grande, Madrid

"Let your subject be Spanish heroes!" Goya wrote to his old childhood friend Martín Zapater.
We have seen the dome of the church of San Francisco, thirty-two metres in diameter, in the distance in the tapestry sketch (pages 40/41). This church was frequented by Charles III and his confessor Joaquín Eleta, who was Franciscan.
This altarpiece shows Saint Bernardino, a fifteenth-century Franciscan friar and eloquent preacher, delivering a sermon to a crowd in front of King Alfonso of Aragon who was a powerful monarch in the Middle Ages. It takes place immediately outside the town of Aquilina. The king and his subjects look up at the preacher in awe as he stands on his rock with a star over his head—just descended from the heavens—like a shaft of light on his face. This miracle star shown during a sermon may relate to the importance of the dissemination of ideas at a time when enlightened people, including perhaps Goya, were keen to express new beliefs. There is no doubt that as Goya rose in reputation, the insertion of his own face brightly lit by a yellow jacket, is in the grand tradition of painters who suggest that their role gives them access to such moments in time—that indeed the artist is a miracle maker as well. The pyramidal structure of the work and the classical building in the background suggest a nod in the direction of the neoclassical style which Charles III enjoyed. But it is ultimately the faces of the people, just normal village people, which capture our attention.
Goya was delighted to have been chosen to be part of a group of several court painters to take part in this commission from the Count of Floridablanca. This did not include his brother-in-law Bayeu, whom he had fallen out with over a previous commission. Goya needed this work as his father had just died and he was now responsible for the financial well-being of much of the family. He was particularly delighted perhaps, because his work at the tapestry factory was drying up due to lack of commissions. The supervisor of the commission was Count Floridablanca (pages 44/45). Goya had to admit to him in a letter that the title of the work was not strictly accurate, as the king in the original story was the Angevin King Renato of Sicily. But Goya decided that as it was a Spanish church it should fittingly have a Spanish king and a great one at that. 6,000,000 reales were approved for this altarpiece, a disappointing fifth of what Goya felt it was worth.

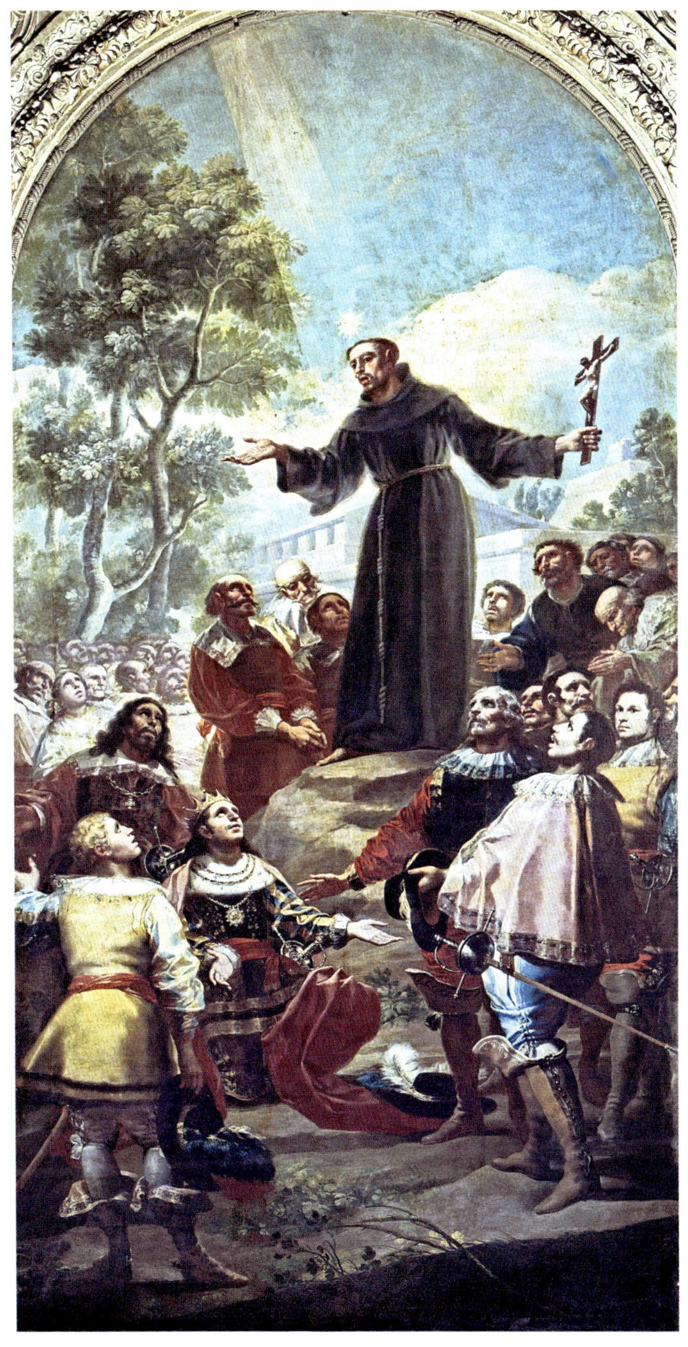

The Count of Floridablanca, 1783

Oil on canvas
262 x 166 cm
Bank of Spain, Madrid

José Moñino was a powerful figure in Spain and for his work expelling the Jesuits he was ennobled by Charles III as the Count of Floridablanca. By 1777 he became First Minister of State. His concern for public service included various important hydraulic projects including the design and construction of the Imperial Canal of Aragon. This provided irrigation across a Spain whose infrastructure had largely been left untouched since the peninsular had become Christian three centuries previously. This official portrait, painted in late April 1783, is littered with symbols by an obsequious Goya who is clearly over-awed by this busy, productive man with steel-blue eyes. His own self-portrait fades into brown into the background as one late evening he presents the count with a painting. We can only assume it is a sketch for this very same portrait. The count, probably far too busy to deal with a lowly painter, takes his glasses to look at it in a perfunctory way, then stares at himself in the fourth wall mirror provided. The count is resplendent in a red suit, a white gold-threaded waistcoat and a sash and white stockings, his hand placed jauntily on his hips. The light falls exclusively on him and, although he was a small man, he is made to look significantly bigger than the painter or his assistant and engineer Julian Bort, protractor in hand. We catch him, the modern man, still working late in the evening, as the clock will tell us, and our eyes are drawn to the papers which are on the table and propped up against a wall. When looking carefully, the viewer can detect blueprints for the Canal of Aragon which the count was working on. The book on the floor is probably Antonio Palomino's *Practice of Painting*, a work highly revered by men of culture of the time. But the final touch is the sharp diagonal from Goya to the count and beyond, where we see the unmistakeable portrait of Charles III, similar to the one executed in 1767 by Mengs (which hangs in the Museo del Prado and is not included here), Goya's mentor. Laden with messages this work is an indication of where Goya's sights are focussed.

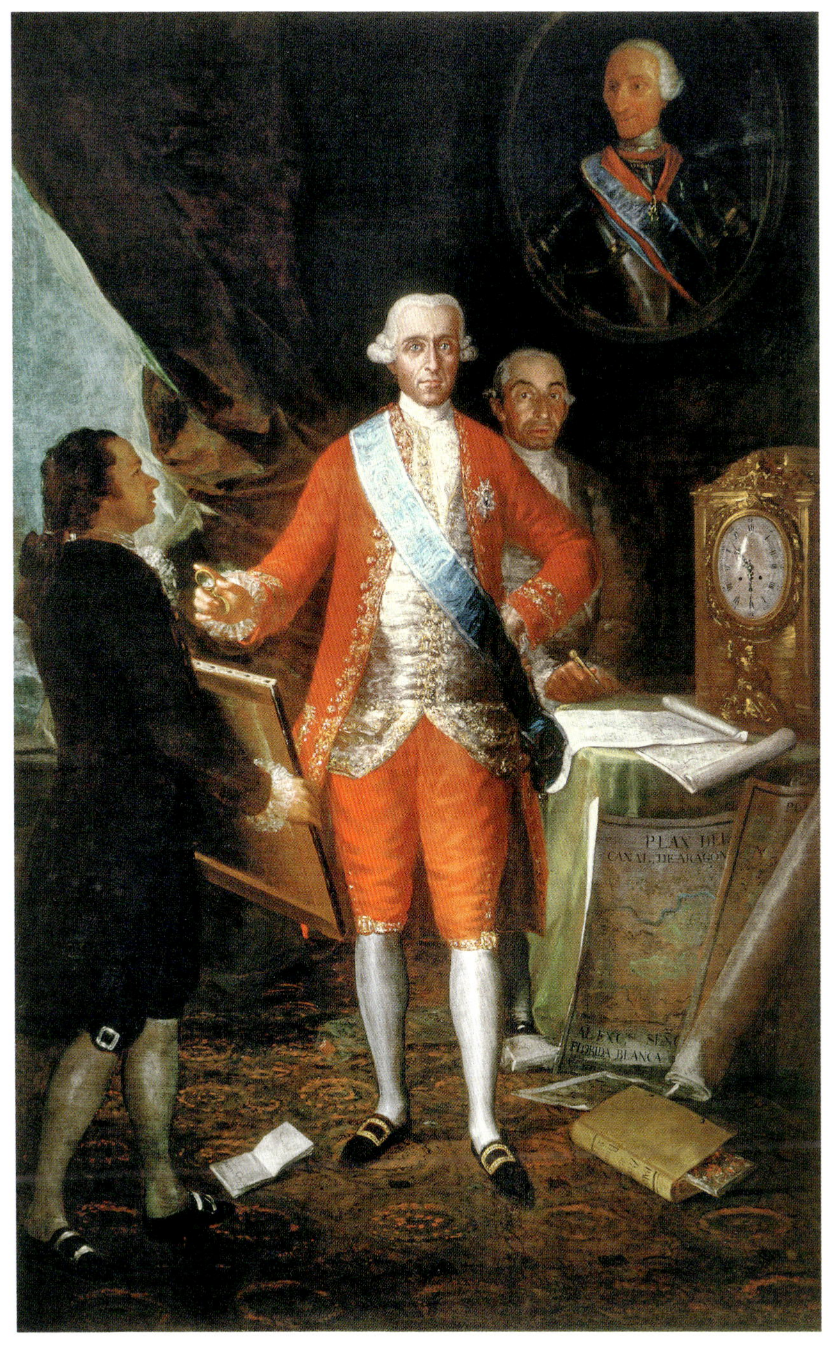

PLAN DEL
CANAL DE ARAGON
AL EXC.° SEÑOR
FLORIDA BLANCA

The Family of the Infante Don Luis de Borbón, 1783

Oil on canvas
248 x 330 cm
Fondazione Magnani-Rocca, Parma

This painting was commissioned by Don Luis de Borbón, the younger brother of Charles III, exiled due to his decision to give up an ecclesiastical calling and lead a more adventurous life as a libertine. We are invited into the intimacy of his home 140 kilometres west of Madrid in Arenas de San Pedro, in Ávila. Indeed, Goya was invited mid-August 1873 and stayed there again in 1784. Don Luis the Infante, now an ageing nobleman, is sitting playing cards, perhaps solitaire, as his wife, the beautiful and thirty years younger María Teresa de Vallabriga—her hair cascading over her shoulders—is being tended to by the barber Joaquin Ramón. He combs her hair before she puts on the elaborate bed caps we see worn by the ladies on the left of the painting. We interrupt an evening in the life of the family chatting, playing cards or having their hair dressed, and Goya plays a part if only on the outskirts as a lowly figure. This is a portrayal of a fun, relaxed evening. Nobility and their servants all pose in a somewhat theatrical way. Perhaps the musician Boccherini was playing for them but now he, like family members and servants, stands next to the man in head bandages waiting for a wig to be made. The children are up late and wide-eyed with tiredness. Especially the little Teresa who peers out at the viewer, hoping not to be sent to bed. (She will reappear in later works.) Don Luis's court became reputed as a cultural centre where musicians could be heard and enlightened ideas discussed. Goya must have fitted in despite his strange presence crouched down at the front of the painting, apparently servile and painfully twisted. But he is included in a portrait of nobility as the virtuoso at work.

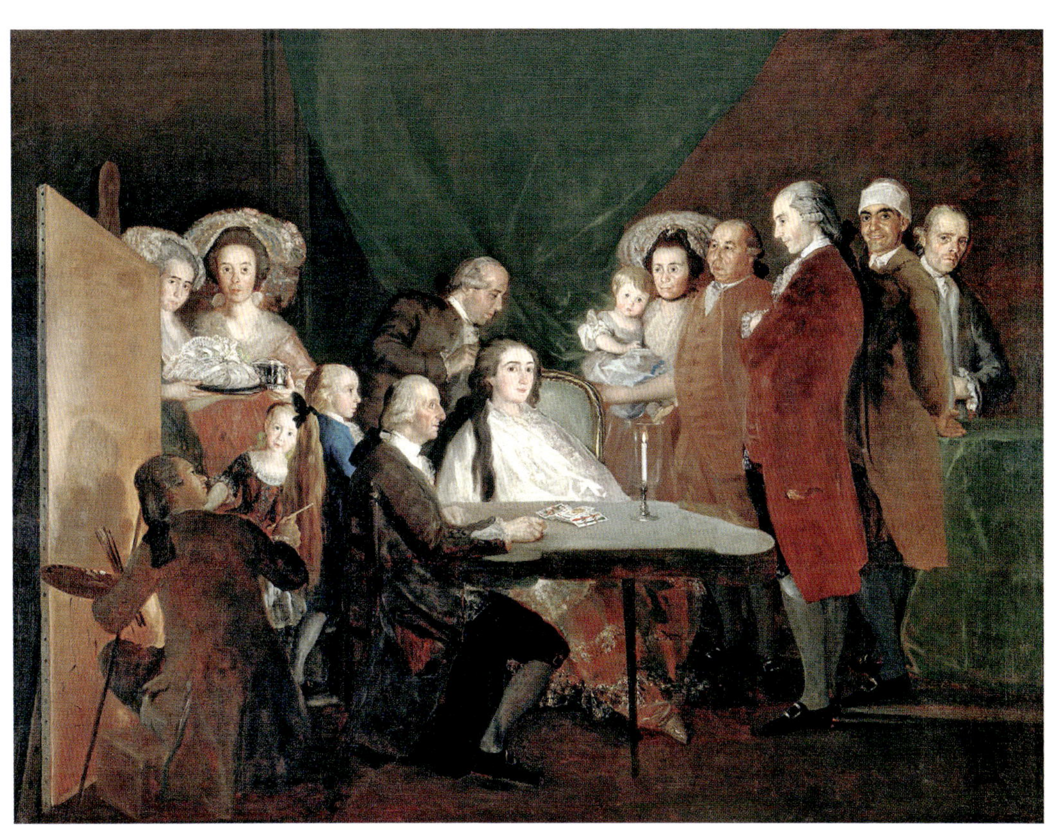

Charles III in Hunting Dress, 1786–88

Oil on canvas
210 x 127 cm
Museo del Prado, Madrid

In 1777 when Goya became director of the Tapestry Works of Santa Barbara in Madrid, he entered royal circles and his career began—a career which would span at least three decades and several Bourbon kings. The first is Charles III who was not an imposing figure but rather a pious despot who liked to hunt. He had no interest in culture or fashion and certainly needed the support of the church and its Inquisition to rule over his largely illiterate people. Did he belong to the elite group of enlightened individuals (*ilustrados*)? Indeed not, as he discouraged educational initiatives and was too lazy to support any much-needed agrarian reforms.

Here we see him close to the picture frame, grinning inanely as he looks directly out at us, his rifle nearly as big as he is and his sleepy dog with the collar inscription "Our Lord the King". King Charles is in his finery, medals and all, but somehow Goya paints him as a bag of rags in an ill-fitting yellow waistcoat, probably made of the finest silk, a tricorn hat and buttoned gaiters. His sashes of the Orders of Charles III, Saint Januarius and the Holy Ghost as well as the Golden Fleece all remind us of the once vast wealth of Spain which was dwindling fast. His little head sits uncomfortably on top of a slightly hunched back. Finery cannot disguise stupidity except perhaps for the sitter. Sumptuous paint itself can blind him. The mountainous landscape around the king—with a variety of undulating greens—lights up this image, softening the impact and drawing attention to the beautiful yellow of the waistcoat, a colour Goya relishes as we will see. An homage of course to all the Velázquez paintings of Philip IV in hunting gear, this painting is not satirical or cruel and the king would have approved of his own commission one imagines, although he died a few months after this portrait, so who knows for sure?

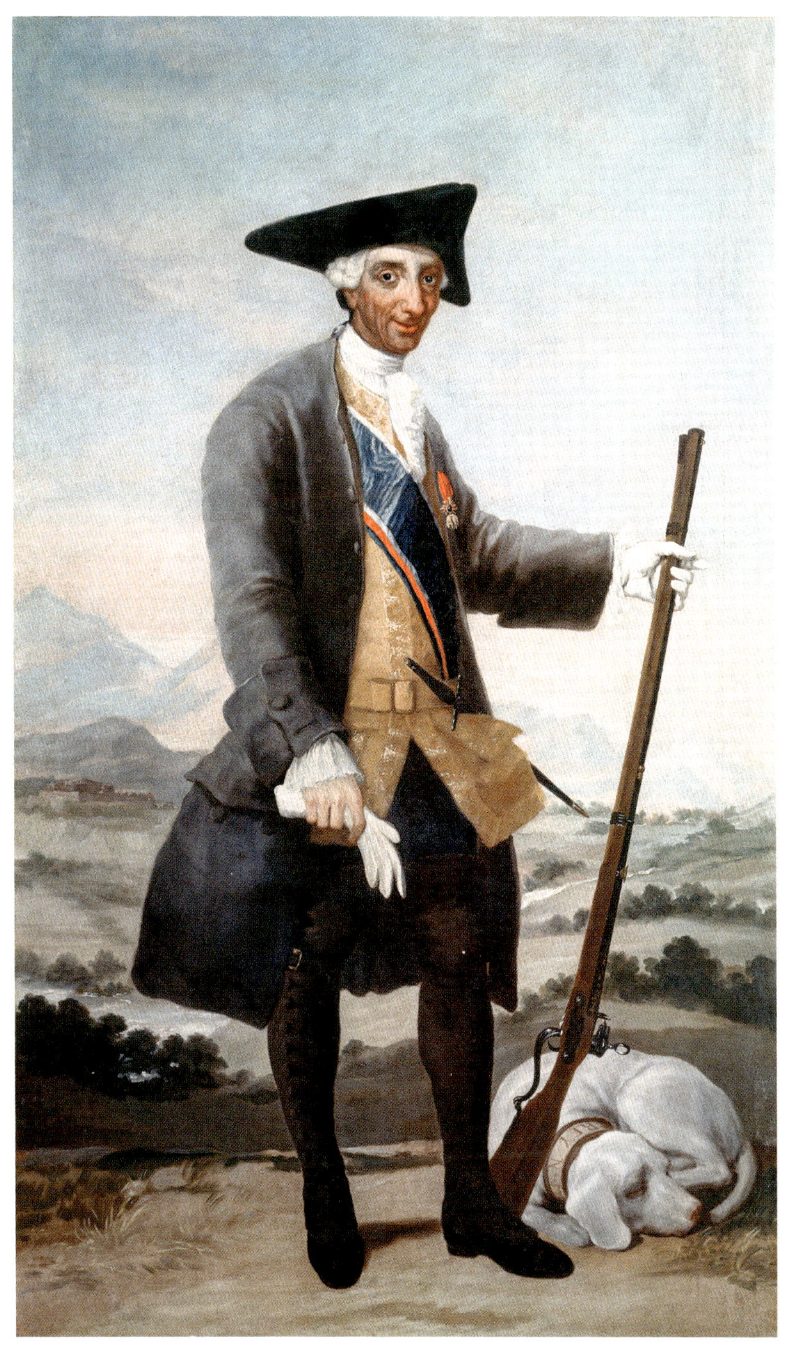

The Duke and Duchess of Osuna and Their Children, 1787/88

Oil on canvas
225 x 174 cm
Museo del Prado, Madrid

Goya, who admitted his first love was hunting, entered aristocratic circles and the entourage of the *ilustrados* via the sport, thereby gaining introductions to some of the great families of Madrid including the Osunas depicted in this portrait. A truly enlightened couple, they were highly educated and deeply involved in the arts. Both were members of the Madrid Economic Society; indeed, the duchess played a prominent role in its Women's Council and owned a huge library containing books rejected by the Inquisition. They maintained a private theatre and were friends with Ramón de la Cruz who wrote *sainetes* and the playwright Leandro Fernández de Moratín, who translated Shakespeare, Molière and more daringly Voltaire. The couple loved music and supported young composers, and the duchess openly discussed the terrible state of women's prisons, the appalling education systems, such as they were and the need for vaccinations, thus drawing some of the finest minds of the time to her home.

This rare portrait shows the family as a closely-knit unit. All stare directly at the painter and therefore at the viewer. The palette is limited, some might say austere, in true Spanish style, harking back, once again, to Velázquez. But the sharp diagonal back-lighting and muted colours bring the faces of the couple and their four children closer. The girls, Joaquina and María Josefa, in grey silk dresses, mirror their mother in style and grace and are holding fans. The duchess wears no make-up or wig, reiterating her status as an intellectual or *ilustrada*. The boys, Francisco and Pedro, are in green unlike their father who, in turn, is in mourning for his own father who had recently died. The Duke seems a looming yet protective figure in the background, sheltering his family. The boys hold attributes, a hobby horse and a little toy carriage on a string. Pedro, who is seated, will later become director of the Prado where this portrait now hangs.

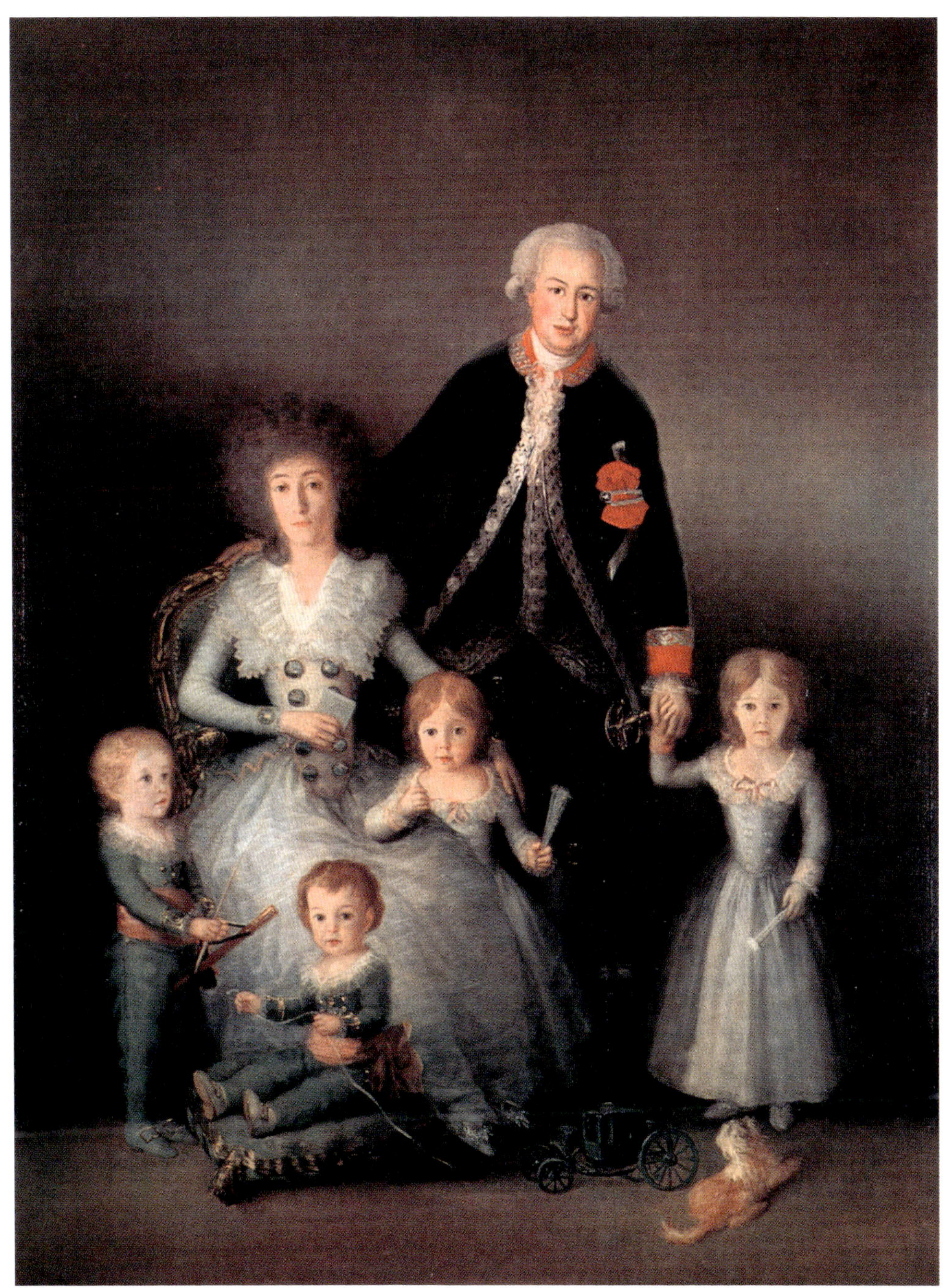

La Pradera de San Isidro, 1788

Oil on canvas
44 x 94 cm
Museo del Prado, Madrid

It is 15 May, the feast day of San Isidro—who was the patron saint of Madrid—where
Goya's family moved to soon after his birth in the sleepy town of Fuentetodos.
According to popular legend, a miracle had occurred in the eleventh century. A man
tilling the earth struck a rock from where water would flow, and the river, called the
Manzanares, would spring and provide water for the city. This water was also said to
cure illnesses, so a site of pilgrimage was created. With time it was more than just a
well or hermitage; so many people came that the event turned into a fiesta, in true
Spanish style.
This small but panoramic view celebrates an early moment in Goya's career and is
a foresight of his many works to come which will celebrate ordinary people. There
they all are, in the sunshine of the fertile ground near the river, drinking, flirting,
the women coquettishly holding parasols or staring into the eyes of their men. The
woman in yellow and red—colours which offset the lush green of the centre of the
painting—leans over to fill a young man's glass. He stares down at her breasts.
This is a youthful painter, painting youth at play. They are far enough away from the
then centre of the city to have the freedom to cavort in the sunshine. We see two
buildings in the distance. The dome of the church of San Francisco El Grande where
Goya is working and to its left, the royal palace of the Pardo which will soon fall into
disrepair.
This could be a sketch for a much larger painting to adorn the royal Pardo, or a
tapestry, but due to the death of the current King Charles III later that year, there
is only this little sketch to enjoy. It is testament to an early stage of a long career.

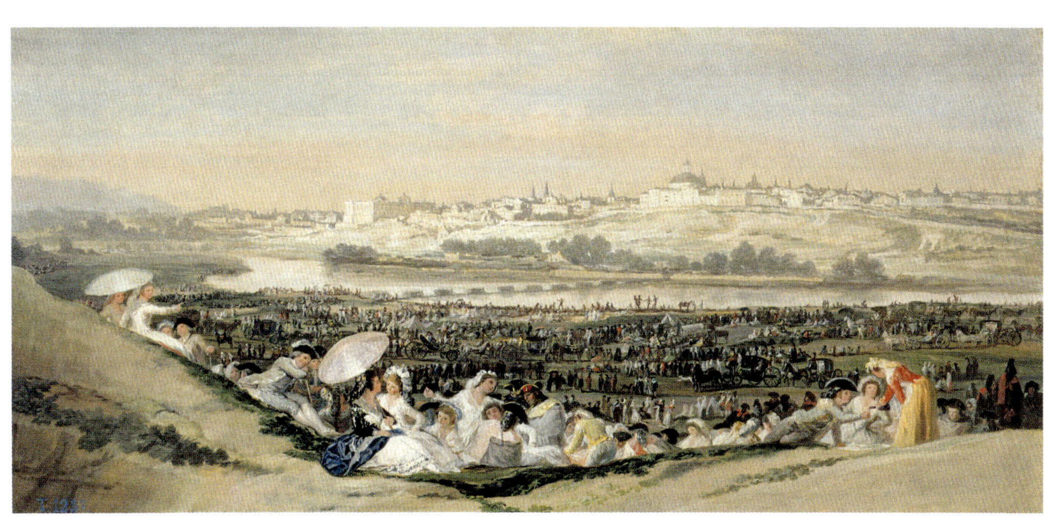

The Wedding, 1791/92

Oil on canvas
267 x 293 cm
Museo del Prado, Madrid

Goya understood the changing role of women during his lifetime. Women beneath their parasols, elegant and coy and resplendent in their silks appear in his tapestries. Others shyly look out from their balconies as if the railings would save them from temptation or marauding men. Bred to marry, if they were 'protected' in their youth, kept pure and unsullied, they could look forward to an arranged marriage with a much older man. Goya's changing representation of women affords us an insight into his times. Like Watteau, Greuze and Hogarth, Goya's view on marriage is spelt out loud and clear. Women are lambs to the slaughter and altar, as can be seen in this work.

We are out in the country for these joyous nuptials and the wedding party has left the church and is making its way back to the festivities. As they pass under a bridge and through a dry river, a clever symbol of a possibly infertile marriage, we are greeted with a smug priest, job done, a piper blowing on his oversized instrument, some naughty kids and women gazing enviously at the beautiful bride. She is young and beautiful and dressed lavishly, although are her shoes are on the wrong feet? In the centre and depicted in bright red is the corpulent groom, presented as an oblivious buffoon—an unlikely choice for the young woman. His thick set features, voluptuous lips and stubby nose suggest he is of mixed blood, probably an heir of a Spanish colonist who had made his fortune in the New World and therefore a good catch for a provincial girl. Look at the group and you will find many gossiping as they walk. They may be envious of this marriage, but they do not envy her future with this husband, nor his with her.

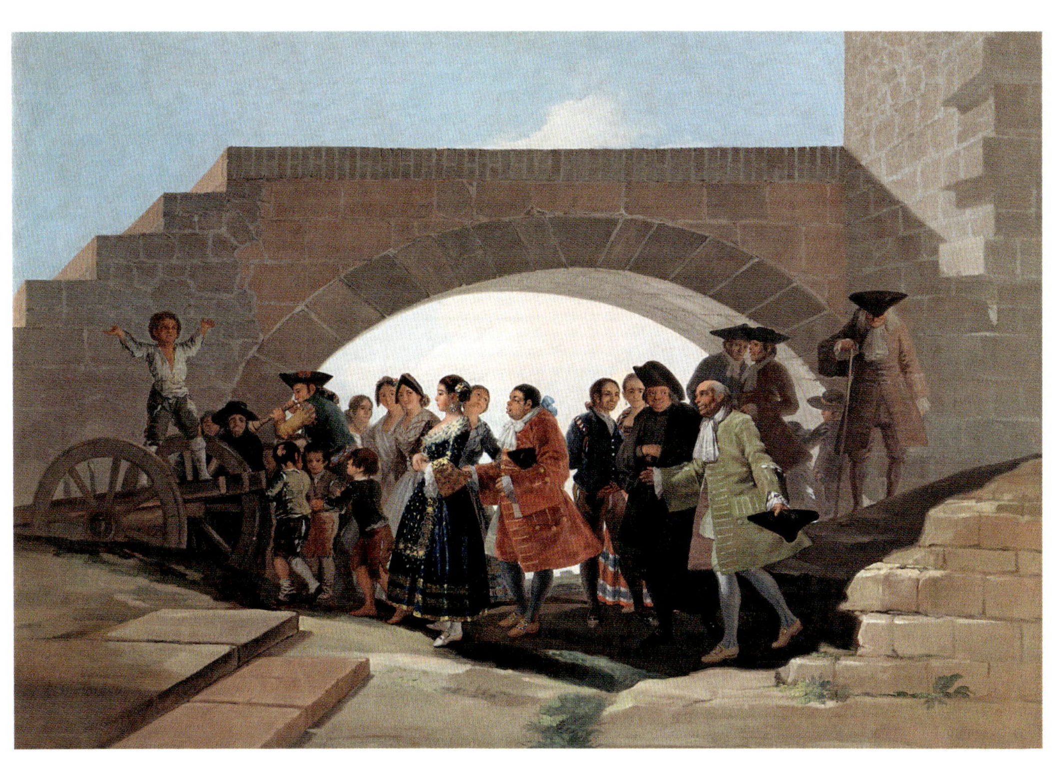

Sebastián Martínez y Pérez, 1792

Oil on canvas
93 x 67 cm
The Metropolitan Museum of Art, New York

At some moment in 1792 Goya fell ill and, at the age of forty-six, lost his hearing.
As the letter which this sitter is holding testifies, Goya was a friend of Martínez
y Pérez and went to stay with him around the time of his illness, perhaps to
recuperate. Whatever the case, Goya must have been profoundly grateful to this
astute businessman, who, by exporting sherry and wine, was able to invest in art.
We do not know exactly what he owned as some works were attributed to greats
like Velázquez, Murillo, Titian, Rubens and others, but we do know that he owned a
number of prints which Goya was able to copy from during his convalescence.
This spectacular portrait is testimony to his affection for this man. The sitter's direct
gaze, long nose and firm unsmiling lips show that he is calm and composed and the
kind of person one might want to be around to help and deal with the frightening
and isolating consequences of deafness. The dark background serves once again to
bring the features of the face into sharp relief as well as highlighting the green jacket
and Goya's favourite yellow trousers with their simple, elegant buttons. The painter's
incredible ability to juxtapose various textures is striking. The white gauze at the
sitter's neck, the green jacket with its brown folds and the bright silky yellow at the
base of the picture all underline the composure and dignity of Sebastián Martínez y
Pérez.

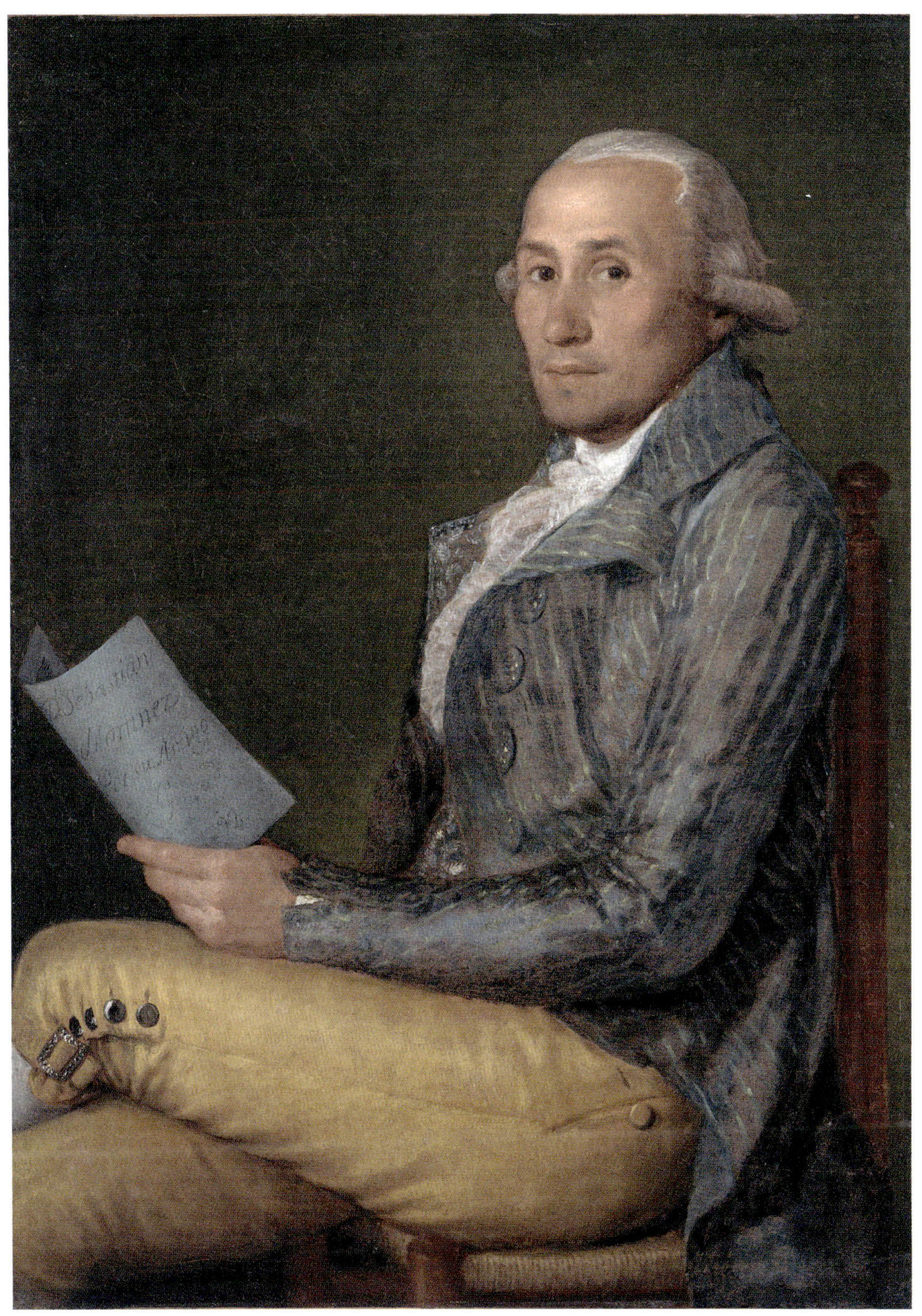

Yard with Lunatics, 1793/94

Oil on tin-plated iron
43.8 x 32.7 cm
Meadows Museum, Dallas

It is hardly surprising that as Goya adapted to his own carceral, silent world he painted late eighteenth-century prisons and madhouses. Dark hunched figures are silhouetted against a slightly lighter doorway and a grey, twilight sky casts its gloom over them. Inmates from the Hospital of Our Lady of Grace have been let out of their cells for perhaps a precious hour of freedom. Prisons were bad enough in these times but the treatment of the mentally disturbed was even worse. There was no possibility of rehabilitation, so men and women were thrown into a pit and forgotten. Or not quite. A further horror was to watch these poor wretches suffer. People even went to visit them in asylums, to gawp at their 'antics'. Goya will address this subject more than once and write about a visit he made to the madhouse in Zaragoza, perhaps to visit a couple of relatives who had been incarcerated. Places for the mentally disturbed were rare in Spain at this time and the existence of a yard (*corral*), latrines and solitary rooms was unusually humane. This scene shows two naked men fighting like animals in the depressing penumbra while others cheer at the back or turn away disturbed. One imagines the figure on the right is rocking himself and moaning as he hugs his arms around his chest, or is he just shivering in his tunic? A warden looks on in despair. All of this is as difficult for the viewer to behold as it would be for an unlikely audience. There are just hints of flesh, a back, a leg, a buttock, a thigh, as if these limbs are separate from the bodies they are attached to. One wonders whether Goya feels some sympathy with these poor souls in their dank purgatory and whether these figures will later populate his *Black Paintings*.

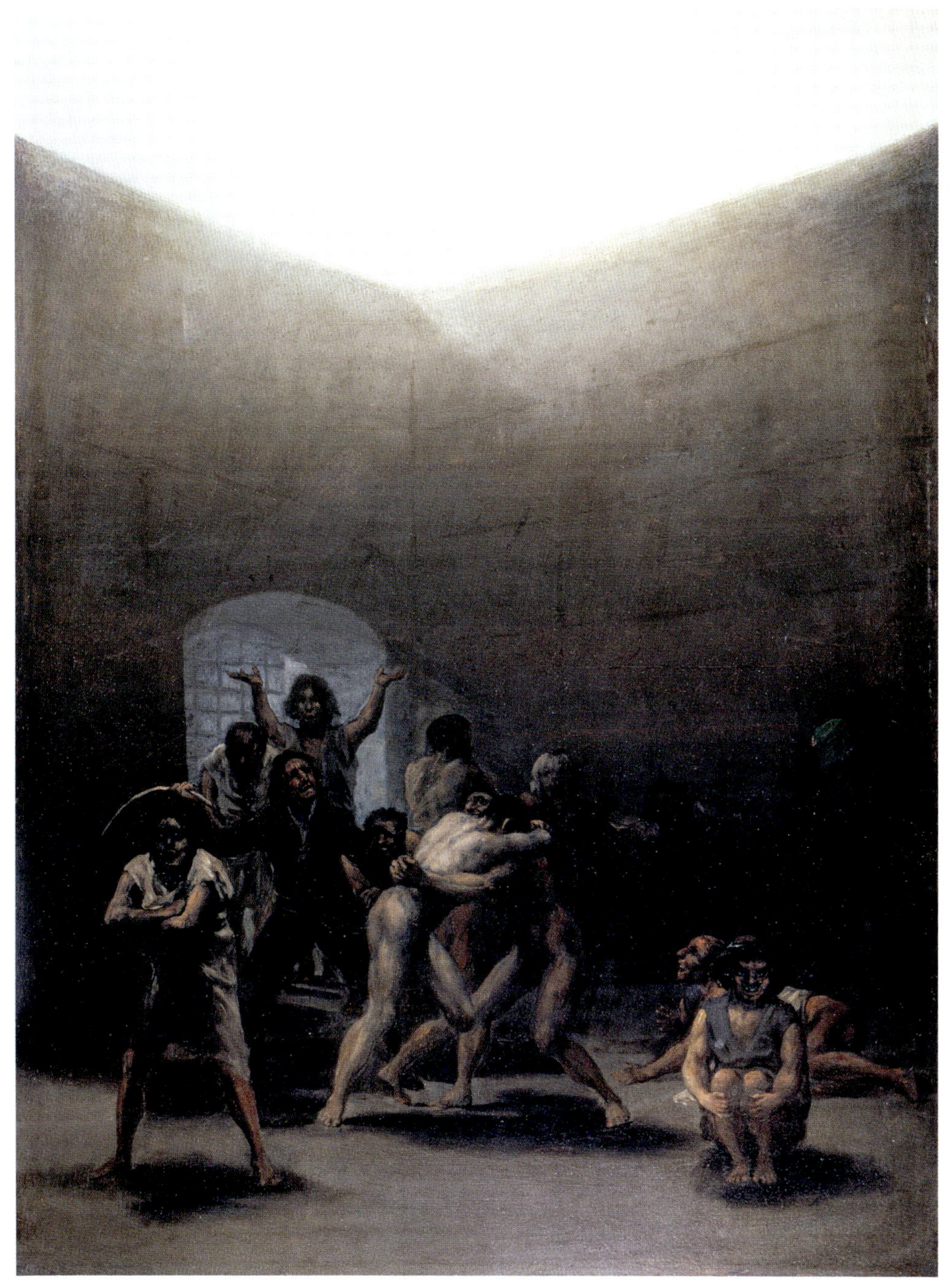

Self-Portrait in the Studio, 1794/95

Oil on canvas
42 x 28 cm
San Fernando Royal Academy of Fine Arts, Madrid

In the 1790s, as both Director of Painting at the San Fernando Royal Academy of Fine Arts in Madrid and the king's Chief Painter, Goya was concerned with artistic status and individual freedom. In *Self-Portrait in the Studio* Goya's face emerges silhouetted against a stark white opaque background. Probably stone deaf by this point he is no longer surrounded by palatial luxury but alone in the semi-dark, shut out from the light in his studio at 1, Calle del Desengaño (Street of Disappointment), Madrid. The street name is rather apt at this low point. With his increasing girth, Goya is a small fat man with a five o'clock shadow, tousled yet wearing a costume which resembles that of a matador or a *majo*. Ever enigmatic, he peers at the unseen viewers, as if they were his mirror. Brooding and unsmiling, with his long hair tied back and sporting an over-elaborate jacket, we wonder why Goya has not dressed himself as a painter. His pot hat with its candle holders stuck in the brim are reminders of his need for light when working and suggests that it is nighttime although it is clearly high noon. The studio seems more like a cell to escape from than a buzzing place of work. We see both the frank incredulity of an aging face and disappointment in his own fragility. A self-portrait is an autobiographical description of a true likeness, if that is possible, and Goya, standing in the dazzling light from the window, does not shy away from the self which may seem ludicrous or self-pitying. It is hard to paint inner solitude or introspection and Goya's tense inquiring gaze challenges the viewer to judge him. The paper and the expensive silver ink stand on the table are reminders that he can pour out his secret thoughts in his letters. Indeed, one of his letters to Martín Zapater, dated August 1800, contains a caricature self-portrait with *Así Estoy* (so you find me) written beside the seated figure with exaggerated lips. By this point he had become adept at lip reading, so this may well be a wry comment on his state.

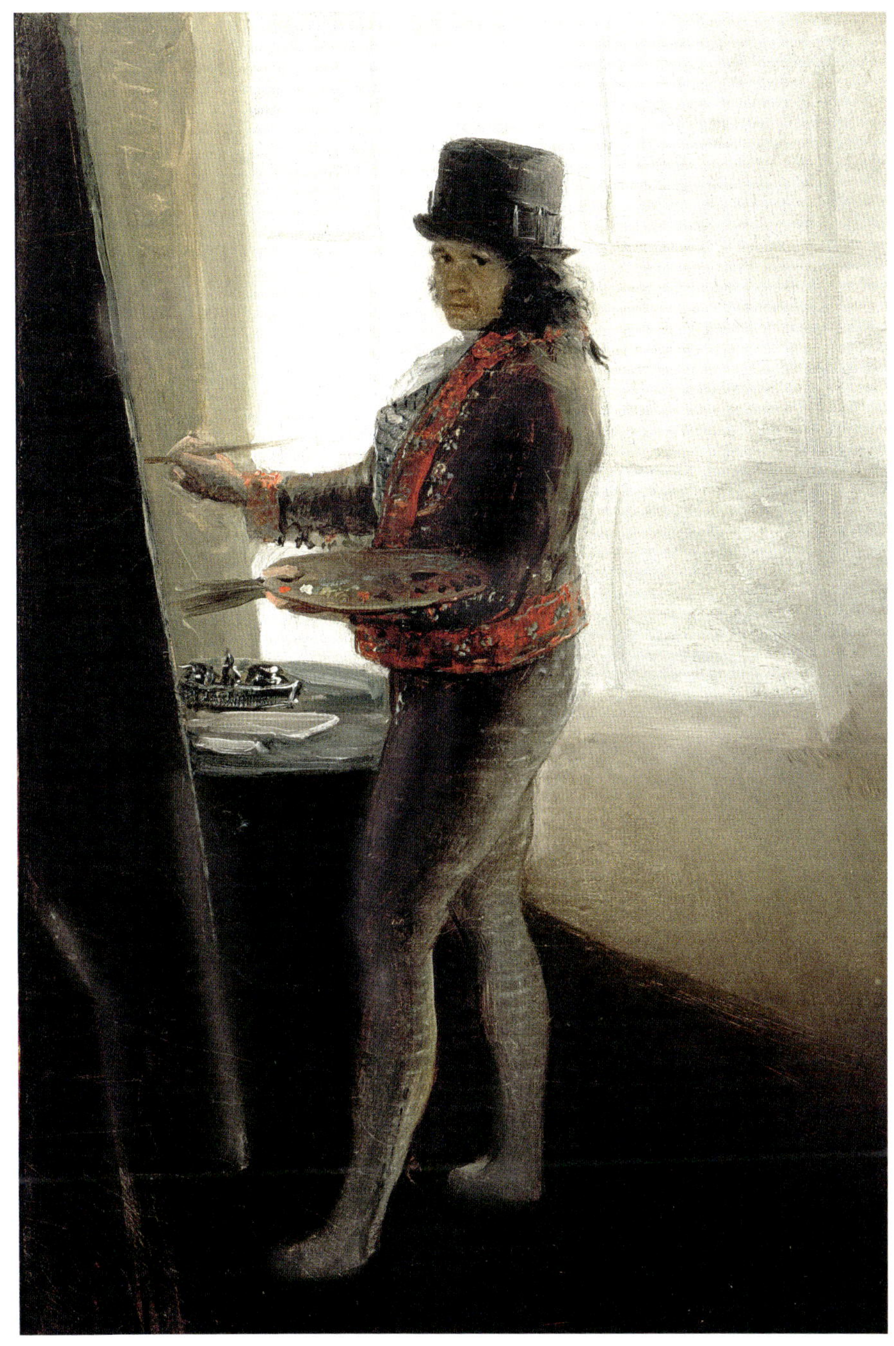

María del Pilar Teresa Cayetana de Silva Álvarez de Toledo, 13th Duchess of Alba, 1795

Oil on canvas
194 x 130 cm
Liria Palace, Madrid

Raised in the small town of Piedrahita, granddaughter of the twelfth Duke of Alba and soon to become the thirteenth Duchess of Alba upon his death, María Teresa Cayetana de Silva grew up in a grand palace with extensive grounds and was educated by the duke who was an *ilustrado*. By 1775, at the age of thirteen, she was married off to the Marquess of Villafranca, possibly to ground her wild spirits. By the time of this portrait, she is thirty-three and a great beauty, a *Maja*. This is a word with a certain connotation in Spanish, describing young people who dress in typically Spanish style and get involved in street-life entertainment. During the Enlightenment, these traditional costumes had been supplanted by French fashion, so María Teresa wore mantillas as well as sashes to exaggerate her tiny waist and she left her hair unpowdered and free, often ribboned—it was a kind of fashion to mark a free spirit and display chauvinistic pride.
Goya fell under the duchess's spell from the moment she arrived in his studio asking him to paint her face. There is some doubt about when she asks this of him, but it certainly suggested an intimacy which was to continue. Her large flashing eyes, unruly hair and small waist did not go unnoticed in Madrilenian society and one of her lovers was Godoy—the finance minister whose relations with Queen María Luisa were also an open secret, making the two women arch-rivals. A foretaste of portraits to come, María Teresa points down with her right hand to the sandy ground where Goya has signed the portrait. Her gaze is implacable, her jewellery ostentatious and her dog, with the bow around his leg, frankly ridiculous. A renowned beauty, Goya seems to mock her bows and her likeness to her dog with gently irony, but the real beauty of this portrait is the painter's ability to capture the texture of the dress accentuating her waist, breasts and body.

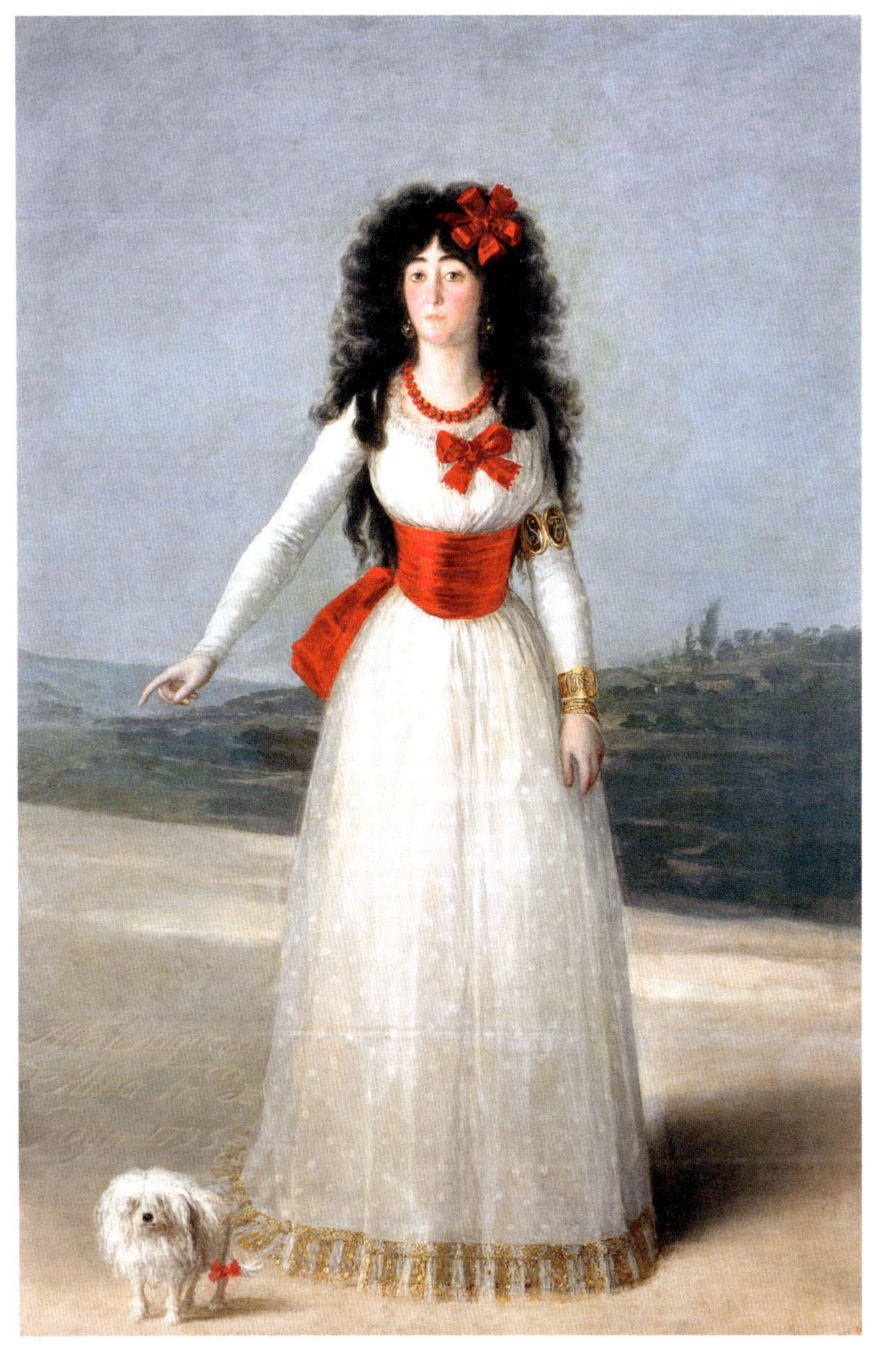

Duchess of Alba , 1797

Oil on canvas
210.2 x 149.3 cm
Hispanic Society of America, New York

This is possibly one of the most enigmatic of all Goya's works. When Goya paints this second full-length portrait of the Duchess of Alba, he now portrays her melancholy gaze, reflecting, at least publicly, the death of her husband. At first glance the duchess is in Andalucía, standing at the banks of the river. Although in black to denote mourning, she is still dressed in *Maja* style with her veil back and mantilla draped across her shoulders. Her gold-coloured blouse, red sash and gold flecked shoes are noteworthy. Is that also a new beauty spot which can be seen on her right temple? Her stance is a reminder of flamenco dancers, her hand on her hip, her head held high, almost aloof and certainly challenging. Looking down from the beauty of her face, the viewer is led via the gold on her arm to her hand, which points clearly to the ground. On her fingers she wears two rings, one bears the inscription *Alba* and the other *Goya*. The extraordinary signature or, better still, inscription in the sand faces inwards, as if for her eyes only. It is of course possible that the duchess did not sanction this work and never saw the boastful inscription suggesting an exclusivity with the painter which was hardly likely. Although the portrait remained in Goya's possession until 1812, the word *solo* (only) had been covered up and was only uncovered by the Director of the Prado in the mid-twentieth-century when it was being cleaned.

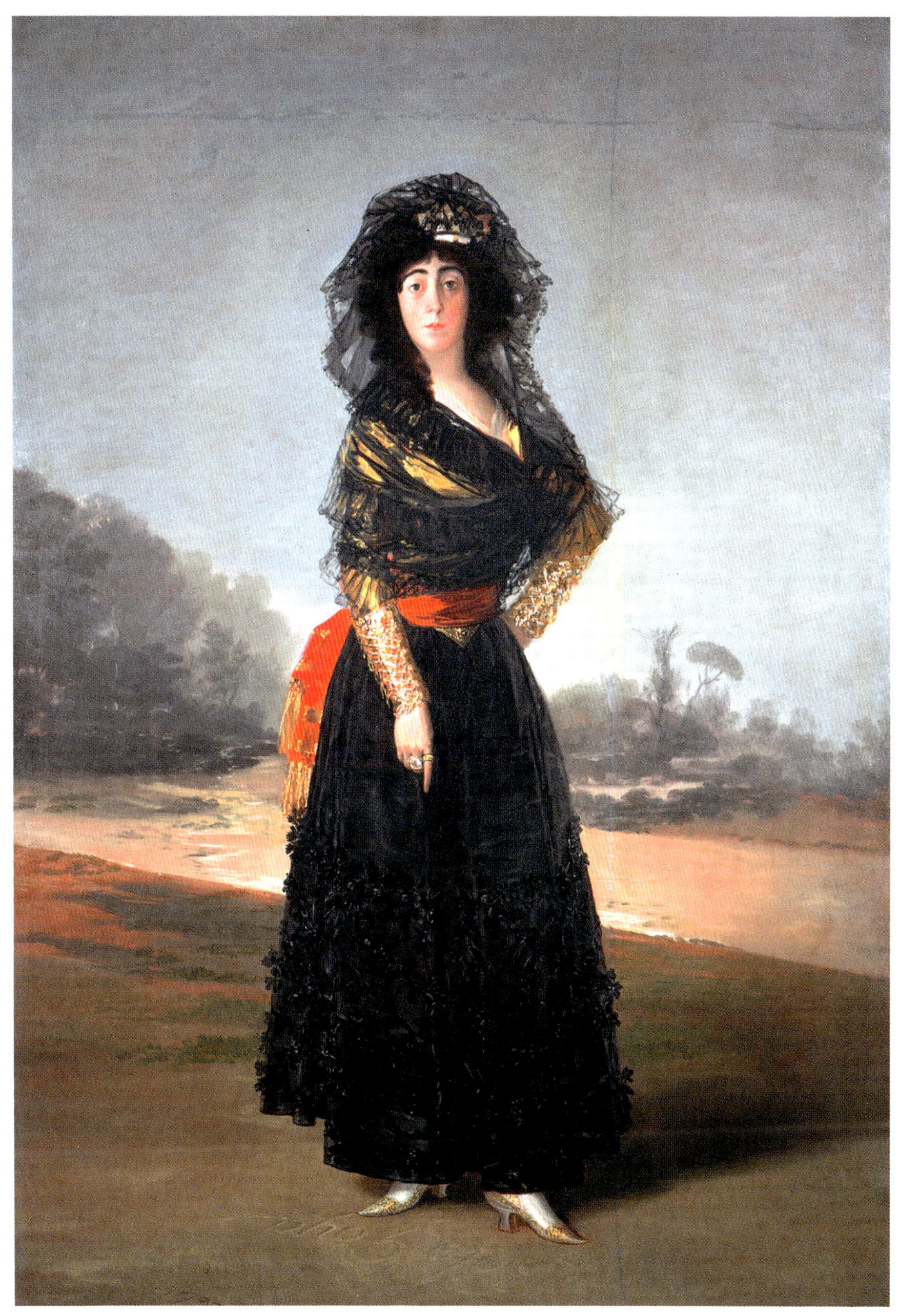

Portrait of Martín Zapater, 1797

Oil on canvas
63 x 65 cm
Bilbao Fine Arts Museum

Goya's childhood friend Martín Zapater from Zaragoza received at least 140 letters from Goya. Through his highly expressive, sometimes crude words and energetically demanding missives we begin to understand who Goya was as a man, not just a painter. It is thus fitting that this portrait of the recipient of his letters should be included in this collection. Sometimes chiding, at other times annoyed, frequently loving and often passionate, Goya tells a sometimes-unresponsive Zapater everything, frequently referencing their childhood together—riding, hunting, roaming the streets and attending religious festivals. Many of the letters are illustrated and some refer directly to the two portraits Goya executes of Zapater (page 30). In one such letter Goya wrote that he would hold up Zapater's portrait to look at and consider him his "soulmate". Zapater is seated at his desk as if reading one of Goya's letters.
In this work the oval frame makes the portrait more intimate. The viewer looks straight into the direct intelligent eyes beneath the bushy eyebrows, of Goya's dear friend, and the painter dedicates the portrait to him using perhaps one of his many nicknames—Marin. We are so close to him we can almost touch his nose, yet he is imposing in his white kerchief and undershirt which lighten his studious face. The hint of a smile crosses his face and Goya makes clear he is respected in society and clearly revered. Zapater was very different to Goya. His parents were landowners and their standing in society meant he could make good connections. Unlike Goya he inherited money and managed Goya's financial affairs, paying Goya's family when needed. In July 1789 he was made a nobleman of Aragon by King Charles IV. In this portrait we sense the trust Goya had in him as well as the huge respect and love he felt for this man.

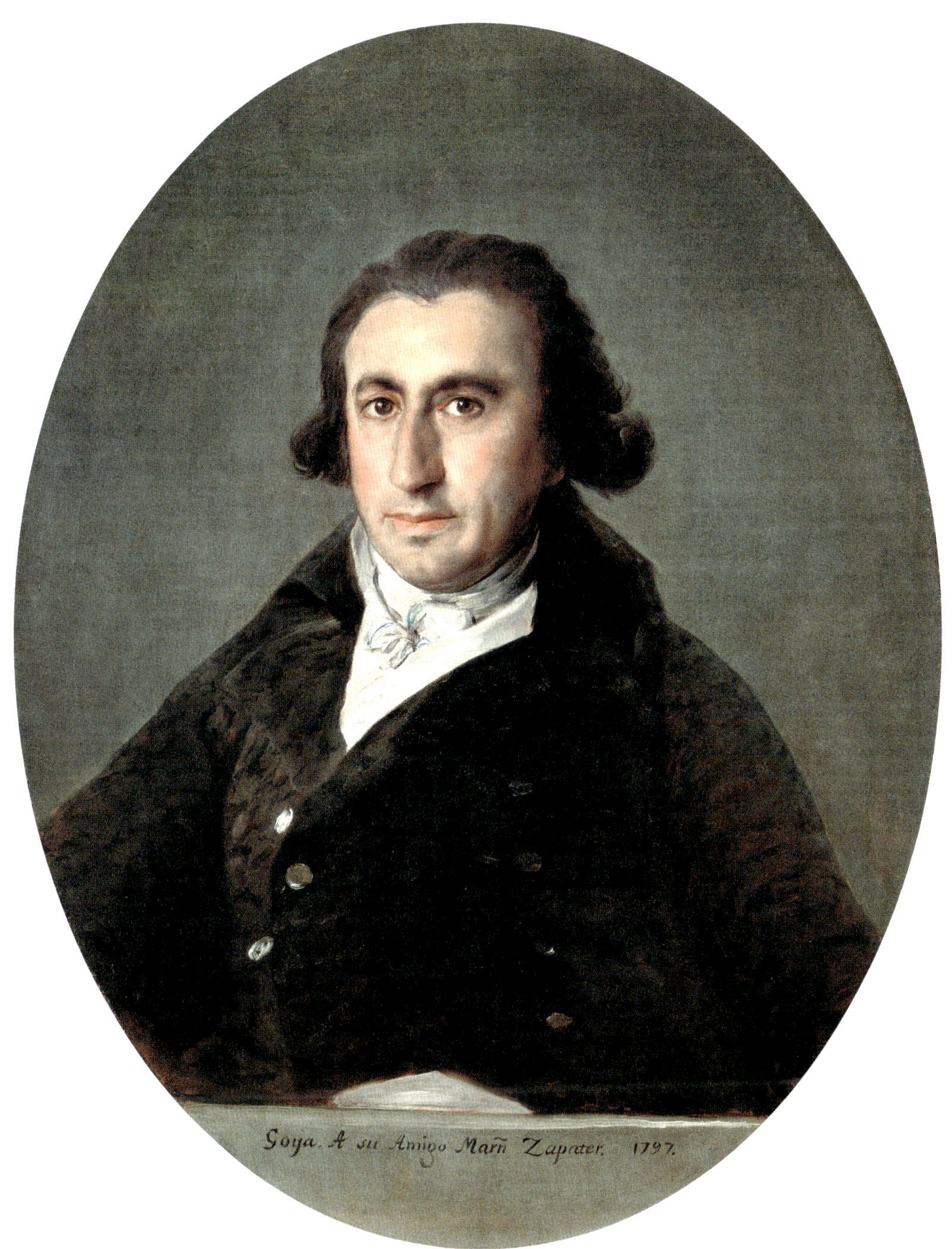

Goya. A su Amigo Mart.n Zapater. 1797.

Por Que Fue Sensible / Because She Was Susceptible, 1797/98

Etching and aquatint
21.5 x 15.2 cm
Museo del Prado, Madrid

In this *Capricho*, (number 32) there are no etched lines. The plight of the woman is heightened instead by darkness and bareness . María Vicenta was eventually condemned and executed in a highly public case in 1798, for conspiring to kill her older husband with the help of her younger lover. Goya's title suggests her innocence; her crime was to be attributed to her youth and sensitivity. *Sensible* in Spanish also means *impressionable* or *susceptible*—so Goya's suggestion is surely that blame could be attached to society for forcing women to marry older men they did not love. She may well have also been cajoled into the act by her lover. María Vicenta is therefore depicted as a victim in her dark, dank cell with its tiny window. She looks down and clasps her knees as she awaits her fate. The folds of her dress, painted with such beauty and liquidity, suggest her vulnerability and highlight her youthful body. There is a hint of an armpit as the dress falls down from her shoulders, and in her despair and loneliness no attempt is made to cover her knees. She will be spied upon anyway through the little window and Goya imagines the leering glances. The light creeping under the door further stresses her captivity and isolation from the outside world. María Vicente is an outcast, shunned by Madrilenian society, despite the latter's salacious fascination with the case.

Goya had done etching before when he copied Velázquez's works much earlier in his career. He knew of Rembrandt and Tiepolo amongst others who were skilled in engraving techniques. Aquatint allowed for hand colouring. Copper or zinc plates were marked or scratched with ink; powdered resin composed of minute grains and speckles—as we can see most clearly in the folds of the dress—created tonal effects and shadows. This work, with its light and dark tones, has a particular beauty despite the horror of prison conditions and the fate of the protagonist.

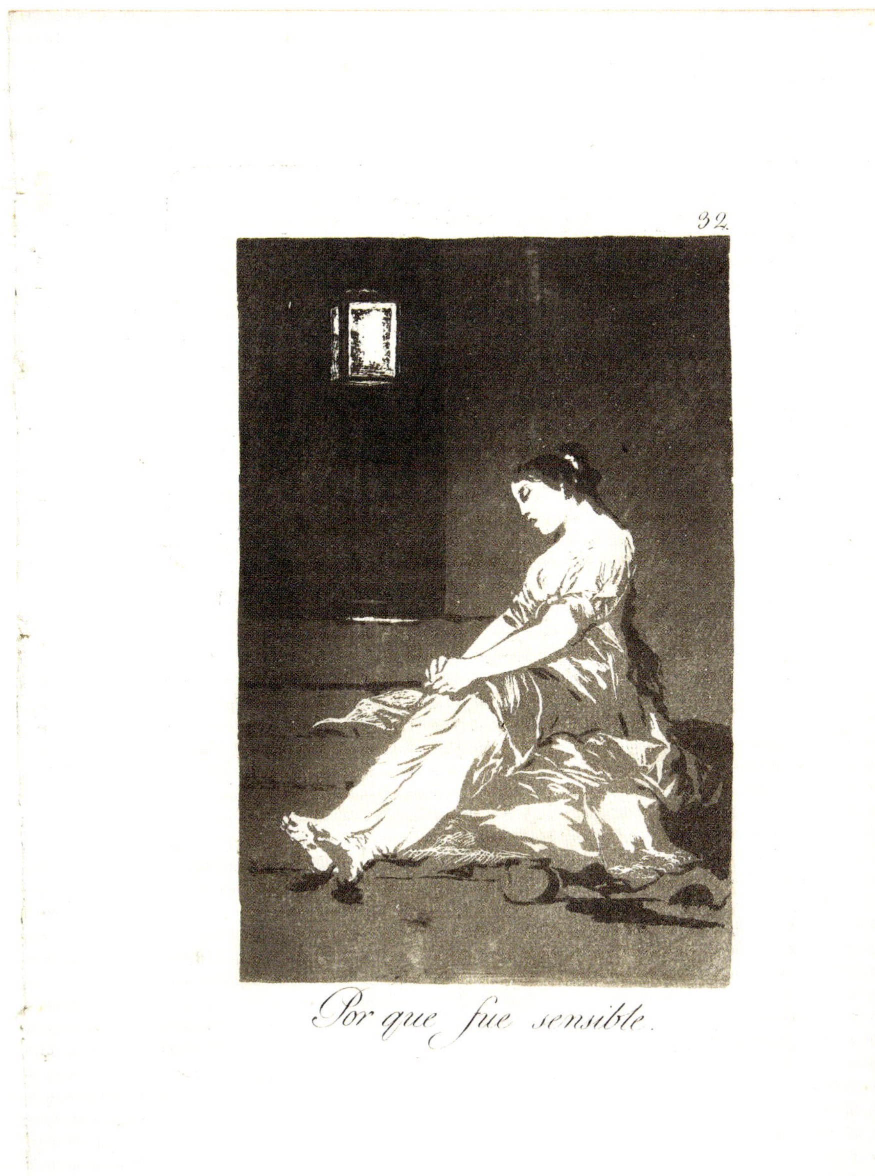

Por que fue sensible.

The Sleep of Reason Produces Monsters, 1797–99

Etching and aquatint
21.6 x 15.2 cm
Museo del Prado, Madrid

The *Diario de Madrid* ran frequent articles towards the end of the century, flagging up the subject of dreaming. It certainly seems that Goya's invention—a word he used proudly—was the concept of the dream as a vehicle for social commentary. In the initial design for the first (later number 43) of his great series of prints called *Los Caprichos*—which roughly translates as whims or fantasies—we observe Goya dreaming or sleeping amongst strange animals, a lynx, a dog, owls, bats with faces like his—grimacing and peering down on his unconscious self. Obliterated in the second version in the medium of aquatint (which we see here), the stuff and the content of his dreams have gone, as have his several faces, replaced with a void. The inscription reads, "The author dreaming. His only purpose is to banish harmful ideas commonly believed and to perpetuate with this work of *Caprichos* the solid testimony of truth". The assumption is that this author is indeed Goya himself; he is asleep and his dream world is laid bare for the viewer to see. This is a clever satirical device used in many of the eighty prints. The medium lends itself to the subject matter and was relatively new in Spain at this time. The sharp black contrasts with the soft wash of the medium, creating an unworldly and caricaturesque feeling. It thereby allows the artist to say what he likes under the guise of the dream, although he vehemently denies satire directed at any one person. Do these creatures signify aspects of Spanish folklore? The owl, wisdom and folly; the bats possible blind stupidity. The evils Goya saw in the then current political climate were corruption and ignorance; and if you are asleep, you cannot destroy such evil. To be an enlightened man, you must banish these creatures of corruption and see as clearly as a lynx. These were cabinet pieces, designed to amuse Goya and not commissioned works.

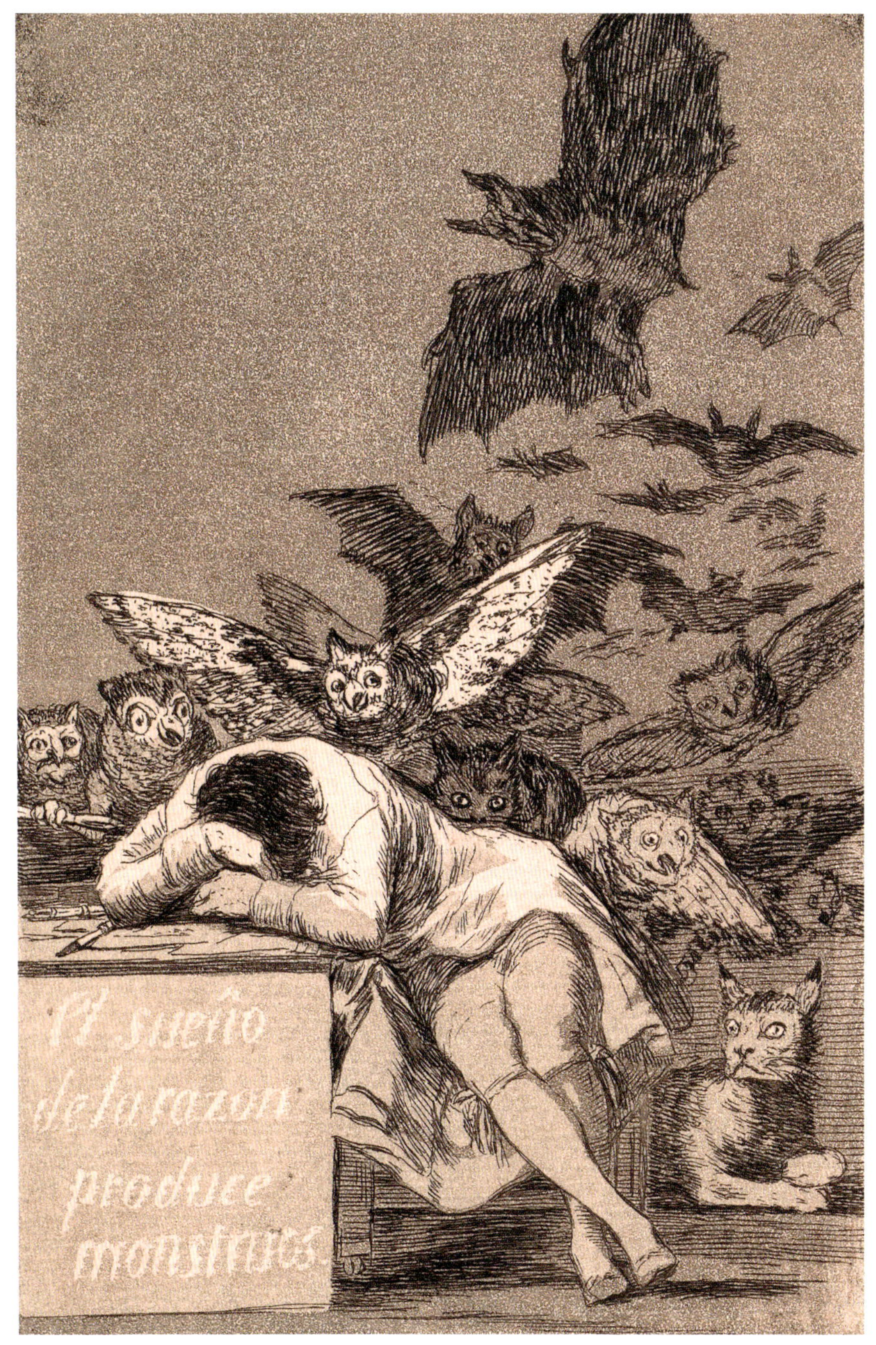
El sueño
de la razon
produce
monstruos.

The Naked Maja, 1797–1800

Oil on canvas
97 x 190 cm
Museo del Prado, Madrid

When Manuel de Godoy y Alvarez de Fario Rios, a royal favourite and two-time First Secretary of State (1792–1797 and 1801–1808) commissioned this work, it was to hang in his private quarters along with Velázquez's *Venus and Cupid* (c. 1650), which had been given to him by the Duchess of Alba. It now hangs in the Prado as part of a pair, although *The Clothed Maja* (pages 20/21) was probably done ten years later. The question has always been: who was the sitter? Was she Godoy's mistress Pepita de Tudó who gave him two children and whom he later married? Or the unlikely suggestion that this was perhaps the Duchess of Alba? Whoever it was, the portrait is daring, provocative and sublimely sensual. Unlike Velázquez's *Venus*, this woman displays her body including pubic hair and splayed, perky, gravity defying breasts, as she stares directly at her viewer. There is no cupid, no mirror with which to play specular games; the veil of mythology has been drawn back and we see warm flesh and blood. Even her feet would have been seen to be daringly naked at this time! Her face is framed not just by her black curls but also by her arms, creating an intimate and serious gaze between her and her viewer.
It is known that Goya was close to the Duchess of Alba from his *Sanlúcar Album* and the time he spent in her home. It is imaginable that he, like many others, found her alluring, but she was to die in 1802 from wasting diseases, so any likeness to her in this picture would have been painted from memory. It has also been suggested that her head does not seem to sit well on the body. Whoever the sitter was, perhaps any comparison was dangerous in the then political climate. It is not surprising that Goya was hauled in front of the Inquisition to explain himself, but the outcome of that encounter is not clear. The hanging of the two portraits was nevertheless suggestive of the decision, as the later *The Clothed Maja* was said to have hung in front of *The Naked Maja* and with the aid of a pulley system the naked figure could be revealed.

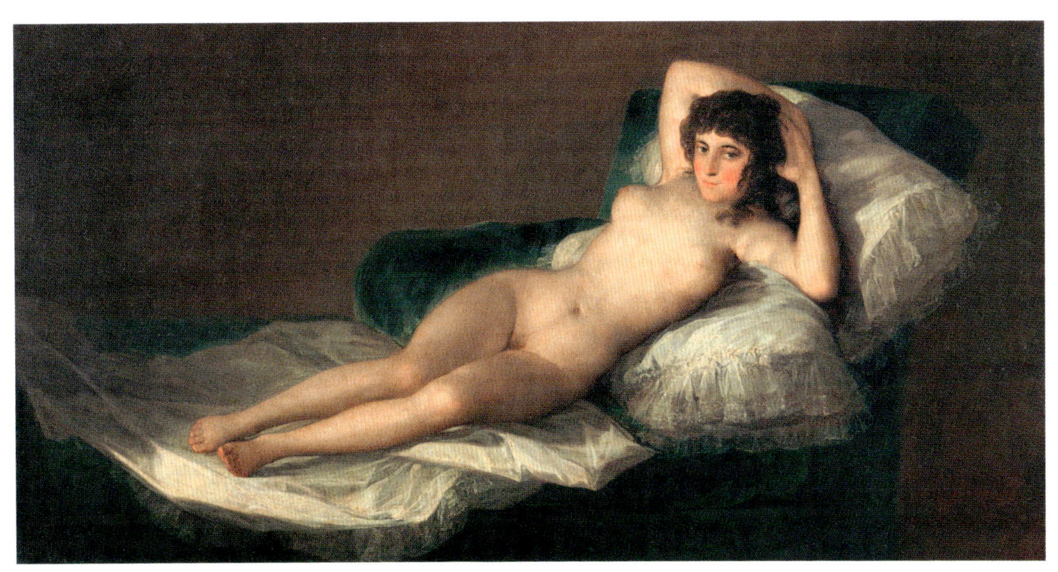

Gaspar Melchor de Jovellanos, 1798

Oil on canvas
205 x 123 cm
Museo del Prado, Madrid

On 27 March 1798 Goya wrote excitedly to his friend Martín Zapater about a coach ride
and a dinner he had enjoyed with the forty-eight-year-old Don Gaspar de Jovellanos,
Charles IV's newly appointed Minister of Justice who was living at the Palace of
Aranjuez. The artist comments that, despite the cold, he was allowed to wear his coat
at dinner, that Jovellanos was friendly and we learn that Goya was duly paid 6.000
reales. The portrait was executed in one of the rooms of the palace and shows the
great statesman, reformer and campaigner Jovellanos, whom Goya clearly respected,
leaning quite casually on an elaborate neoclassical desk with ram skulls and garlands, in
the traditional pose of melancholy—although this pose can also allude to pensiveness,
contemplation and intelligence. The quill is in the ink pot, and paper is also available,
although much of it has already been written on. There is also an open book. This is
a learned statesman who has taken a moment off his work to sit for the painter. On
his desk is a bronze sculpture of Minerva, the goddess of Wisdom, Sciences, Arts and
Industry—all enlightened pursuits. Her right hand seems to point at or extend towards
the sitter as though to protect him, and her shield bares the emblems of Jovellanos's
Asturian School of Nauticals and Minerology. The statesman carries a paper on which is
written, *Jovellanos by Goya.*
The Minister of Justice wears tasteful colours of black and silvery grey which contrast
beautifully with the yellow-gold chair, the bronze highlights on the sculpture and what
seems to be a woven tapestry on the wall behind him. What is rendered so well are
the various textures—the wood carving, the bronze and the shimmering silk of the
jacket. All expensive—these are the accoutrements of wealth which come with success.
Jovellanos, with his serious face, natural, wigless hair and direct gaze, is a man who can
be trusted.

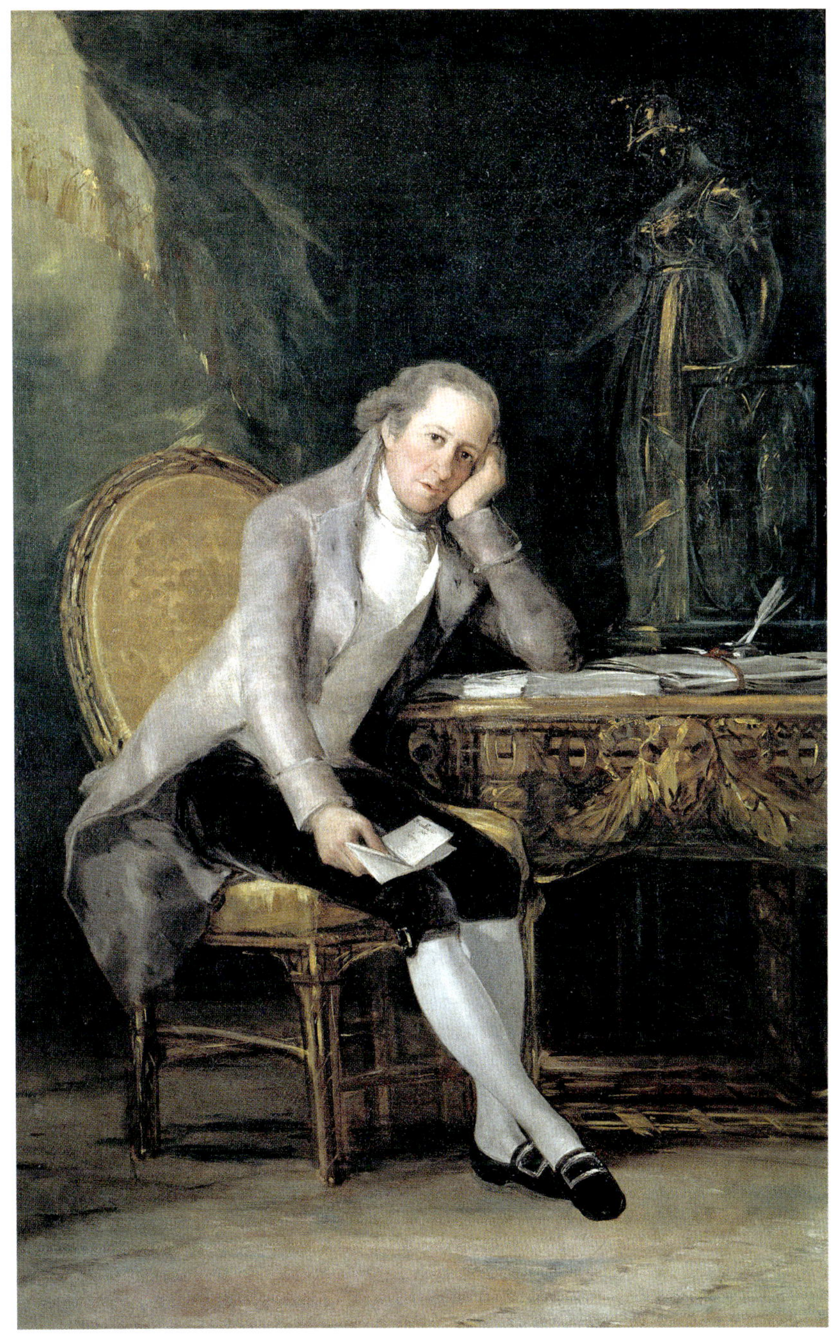

Dome of San Antonio de la Florida, 1798

Frescoes
Church of San Antonio de la Florida, Madrid

The little church of San Antonio de la Florida was known primarily as a place of pilgrimage and stood on the site of one of the old city gates, on the outskirts of Madrid. Today it is Goya's burial place; back then it was an exciting commission, probably facilitated by Jovellanos. It was built by the Italian Felipe Fontana in the shape of a Greek cross and had a dome, supported by four arches which needed decoration. The subsequent frescoes depict the miracle of Saint Anthony of Padua. It should be noted that it is somewhat surprising that the church is dedicated to a Portuguese saint although his cult was widely spread in Spain.
Although Goya must have welcomed the four-months-commission, one can only imagine how hard it must have been for him to climb up on to scaffolding which was thirty-three feet high as he had vertigo at the time due to his deafness. Also, fresco work is slow and laborious, but he needed the commission to shore up his dwindling finances.
The result is spectacular. The story depicted in the dome was compiled by a French priest and translated into Spanish by Fra José Isla. The scene takes place in Lisbon. We see a tonsured saint in brown robes with a pale-yellow halo miraculously raising a man from the dead. Legend has it that Saint Anthony's father, Martin Bulloes, was accused of murdering a man. Anthony is said to have raised him from the dead and asked him directly whether his father was guilty. The resounding "no" is witnessed by all the fifty or so figures near the vertiginous iron railing or balustrade. Some lean on it to watch and marvel, some are not interested and the children play on the railings. The miracle is clothed in the ordinariness of everyday life, while the angels in the pendentives are blonde, voluptuous and secular. How was this work received in 1799? The silence says it all.

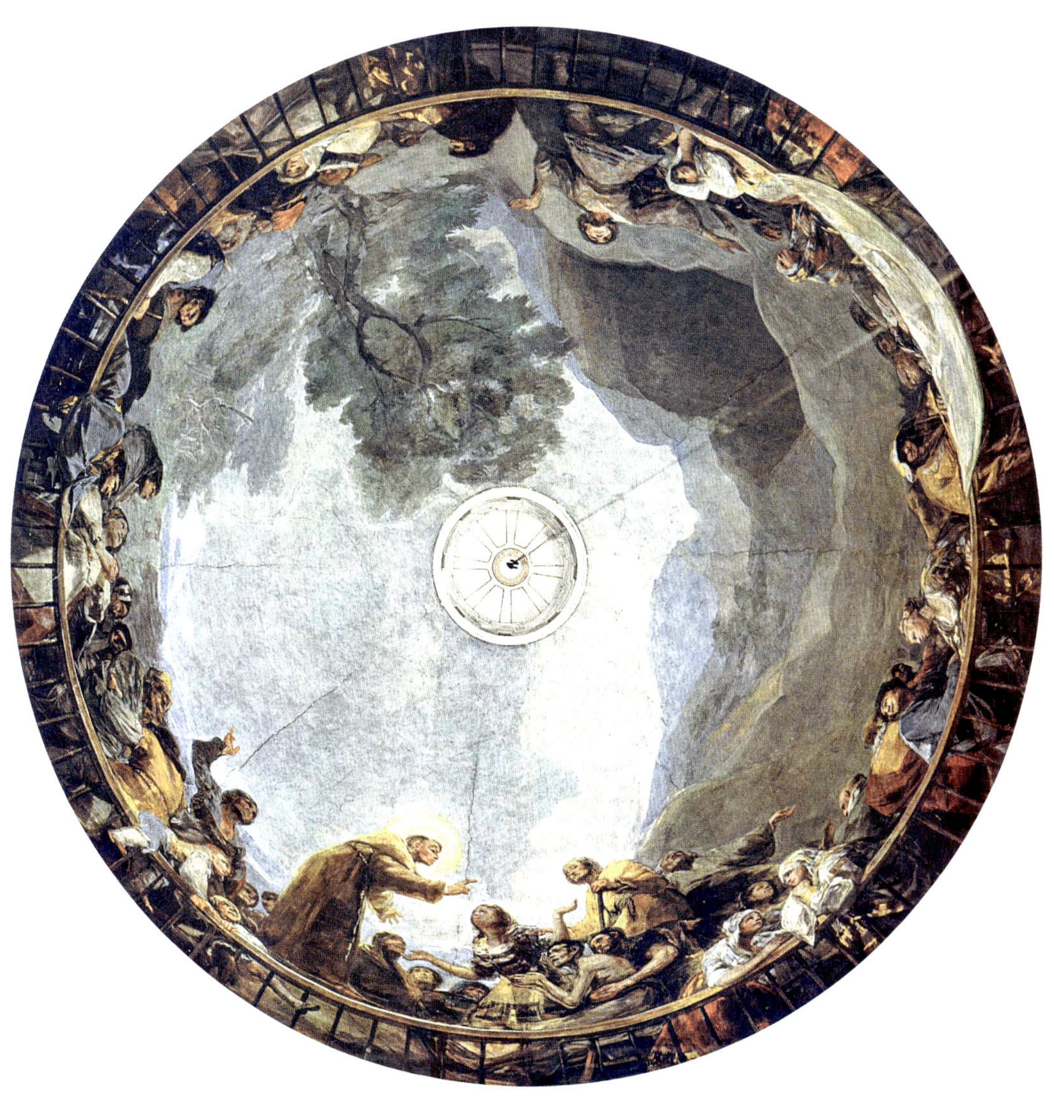

Queen María Luisa on Horseback, 1799

Oil on canvas
338 x 282 cm
Museo del Prado, Madrid

In her letters, Queen María Luisa mentions her horse Marcial who had been given to her by Godoy but proved spirited and difficult to control. Certainly Marcial was a sturdy horse as his hind legs testify. This is a record of her eventual success with him and Goya was clearly commissioned to express this in the way she rides, the perfect angle of the horse's head and the obvious gentle trot. The horse in his best gold bridle is even more elaborately drawn than the queen herself. The monastery El Escorial can be seen in the distant Sierra de Madrid, an emblem of traditional family values. The jaunty hat and red flower, the queen's large saddle which she appears to sit astride and her full regalia all suggest an amiable, modern monarch of the people.

The informality of the title of this work suggests not only the importance of the horse Marcial, which the queen wanted immortalised, but also her own uncomfortable pose. She complained that she had had to sit for hours (two and a half) on a pedestal, not on a horse, which might explain the awkwardness of her position. It is nevertheless surprising she is not given her full regal title, although work titles can often be misleading as they are not always given by the artist. This is one of a pair of paintings of the royals on horseback where Goya emulates the Velázquez portraits he etched in 1778. Traditionally, equestrian portraits tell something about the sitter. With ill-fitting dentures, this portly woman gives a half smile as she looks at her artist with warm, frank brown eyes. Very little is known about her. She had many miscarriages and bore seven children to term. Her son, Fernando, whom she loathed, will be discussed later.

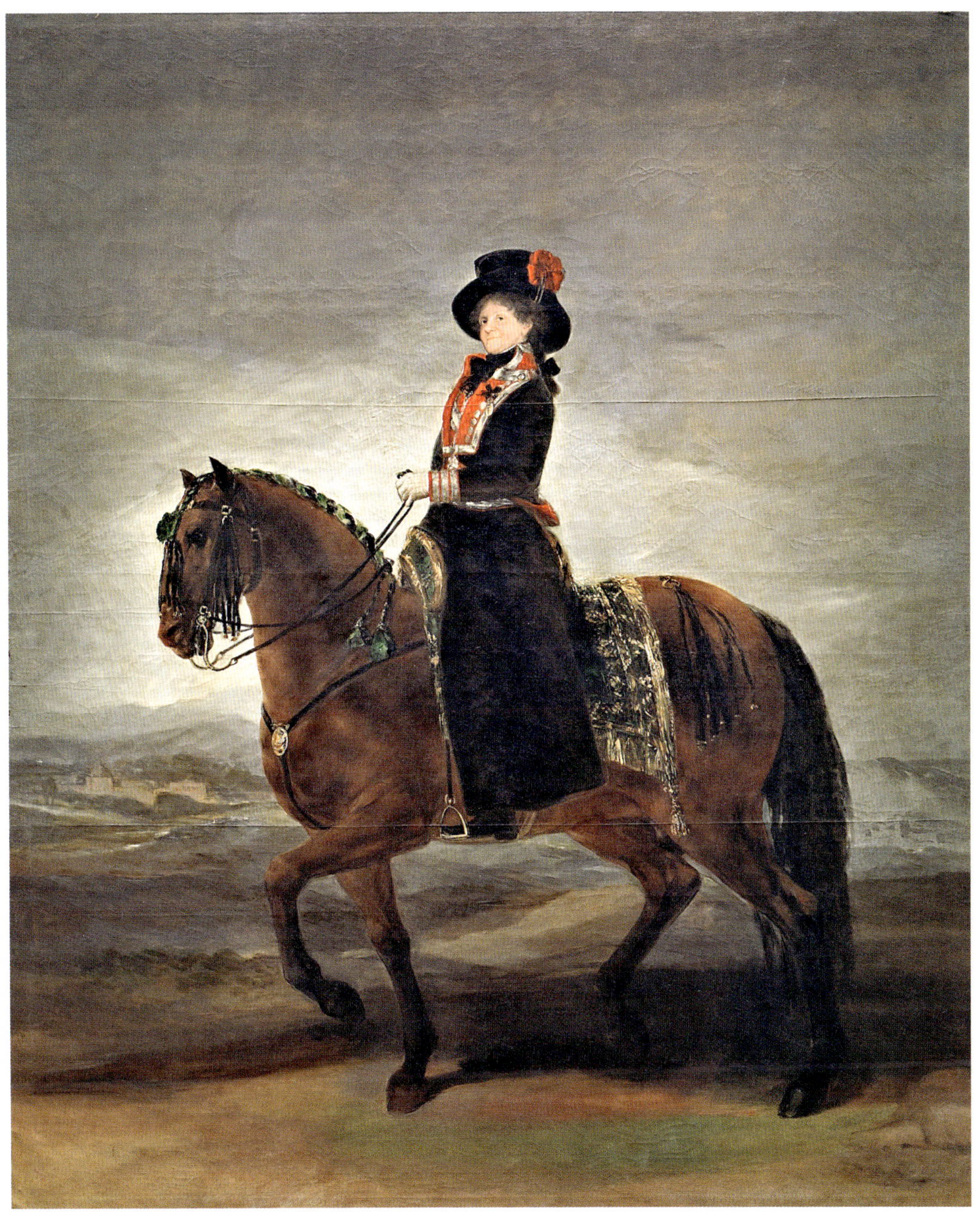

The Family of Carlos IV, 1800

Oil on canvas
280 x 336 cm
Museo del Prado, Madrid

This is a large canvas assembled by workers who had to sew the three pieces together. Goya had just become First Court Painter when he set about one of the most important commissions of his career. Members of the Spanish royal family, life size, are gathered in all their finery. All the males wear the blue and white ribbons of King Charles III and it is interesting to imagine how the touches of gold and silver on the clothes would have glimmered in the original oil lights or candles which lit the painting in those days. Set in Goya's studio, light falls on Queen María Luisa as nurturant mother queen and matriarch, holding the hand of her youngest child, Francisco de Paula and with her arm protectively around her daughter María Isabel. In his timely advertisement for the functional, stable Spanish royal family, citing Velázquez's *Las Meninas* (1656), Goya stands quietly and discretely at the back. A comparison with *Las Meninas* stresses a lack of narrative. All the characters are present—on stage and there to be viewed. The Prince of Asturias, who will become the much-disliked King Ferdinand VII, is also highly lit and dressed in sumptuous blue silk. Beyond him the viewer is led towards a woman's face in the shadows; the future wife of the Prince of Asturias, María Antonia of Naples who is not shown fully as the marriage had not yet taken place. One questions why she is looking directly at the vast expanse of black which is the painting on the left-hand side? Restoration of the painting in 1967 by Xavier de Salas, the then Prado museum director, revealed a painting within a painting precisely where the not-yet-unveiled woman looks. The cleaning exposed a bacchanal consisting of three figures, two are women while the male figure appears engrossed in them. It is clearly Goya himself. "Goya without a doubt", claimed Salas. The Romantic genius, Goya, has portrayed himself twice—as the reticent ever-discreet observer in the shadows as well as Bacchus, the Classical god of mystical ecstasy and artistic and sexual inspiration.

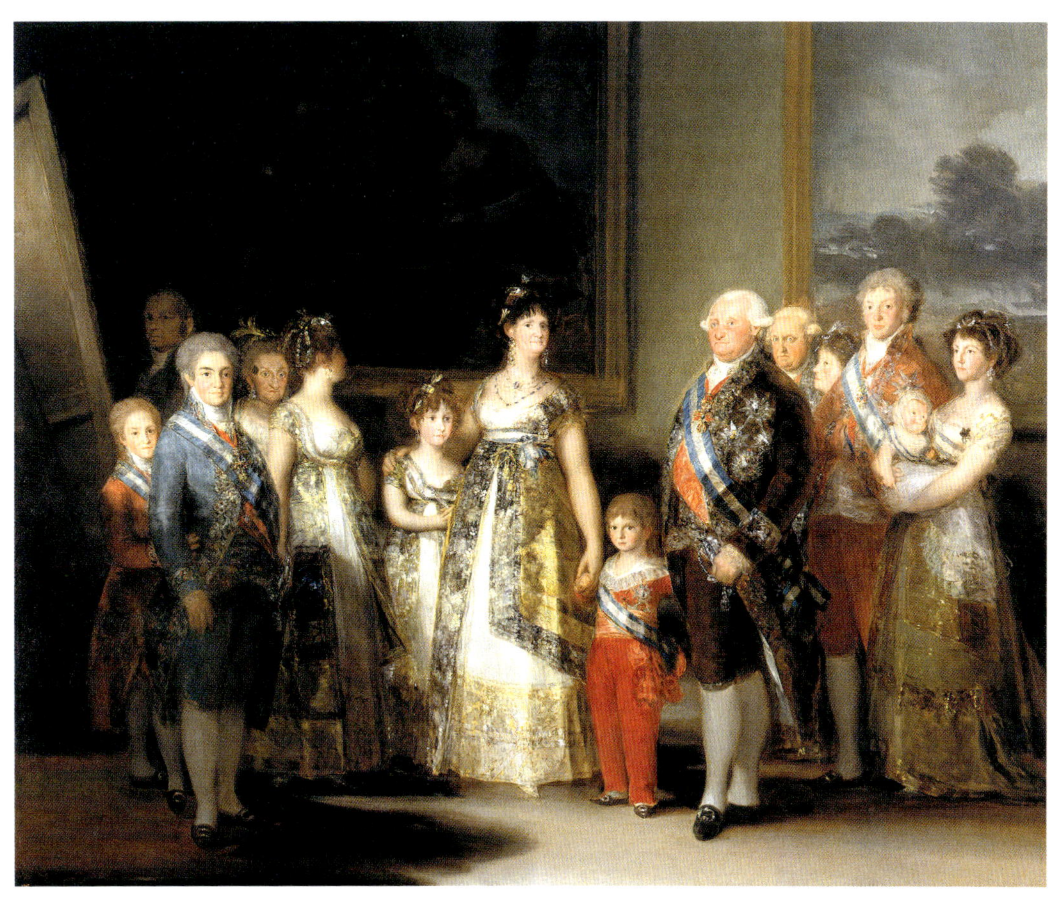

The Countess of Chinchón, 1800

Oil on canvas
216 x 144 cm
Museo del Prado, Madrid

In the painting *The Family of the Infante Don Luis de Borbón* (pages 46/47) a little
girl, the daughter of Don Luis, stares straight out at the viewer. She was María Teresa
de Borbón y Vallabriga, aged two years nine months. She later became the Countess
of Chinchón. Goya will paint the young girl again in 1784, fresh faced and healthy. In
this portrait she is enclosed in the black background of a darkened room, enveloped
in and isolated by her confinement. She is not quite twenty and, due to her family
circumstances, has been married off to Godoy—some say in order to end her father
Don Luis' banishment allowing him to re-enter court circles, others say that the
queen, who also loved Godoy, was jealous of his new relationship with Pepita Tudó
and found him a wife. After years in a convent, she now sits at a slightly uncomfortable
angle on a carved and gilded armchair. Her dress and bonnet are made of the finest
silks and gauzes in the French high-waist fashion, but all the riches in the world will
make no difference to her sad eyes and unsmiling lips. The air of melancholy is further
enhanced by her unruly curls and the wheat sprigs at her bonnet, which Godoy
himself openly mocked. She is pregnant once again after two miscarriages. The folds
of her dress enable us to see her swelling stomach, and the sense of her vulnerability,
shyness and defencelessness is thus enhanced even more, as she looks away from
the viewer. Her bare arms show deference to courtly styles as the queen herself was
said to be proud of them; and her hands are clasped nervously, displaying the family
rings and a miniature portrait of Godoy.
We feel Goya's sympathy for her in an image which seems to glow, the light firmly
radiating from such a wan figure. This is one of the most tender portraits Goya will
ever execute.

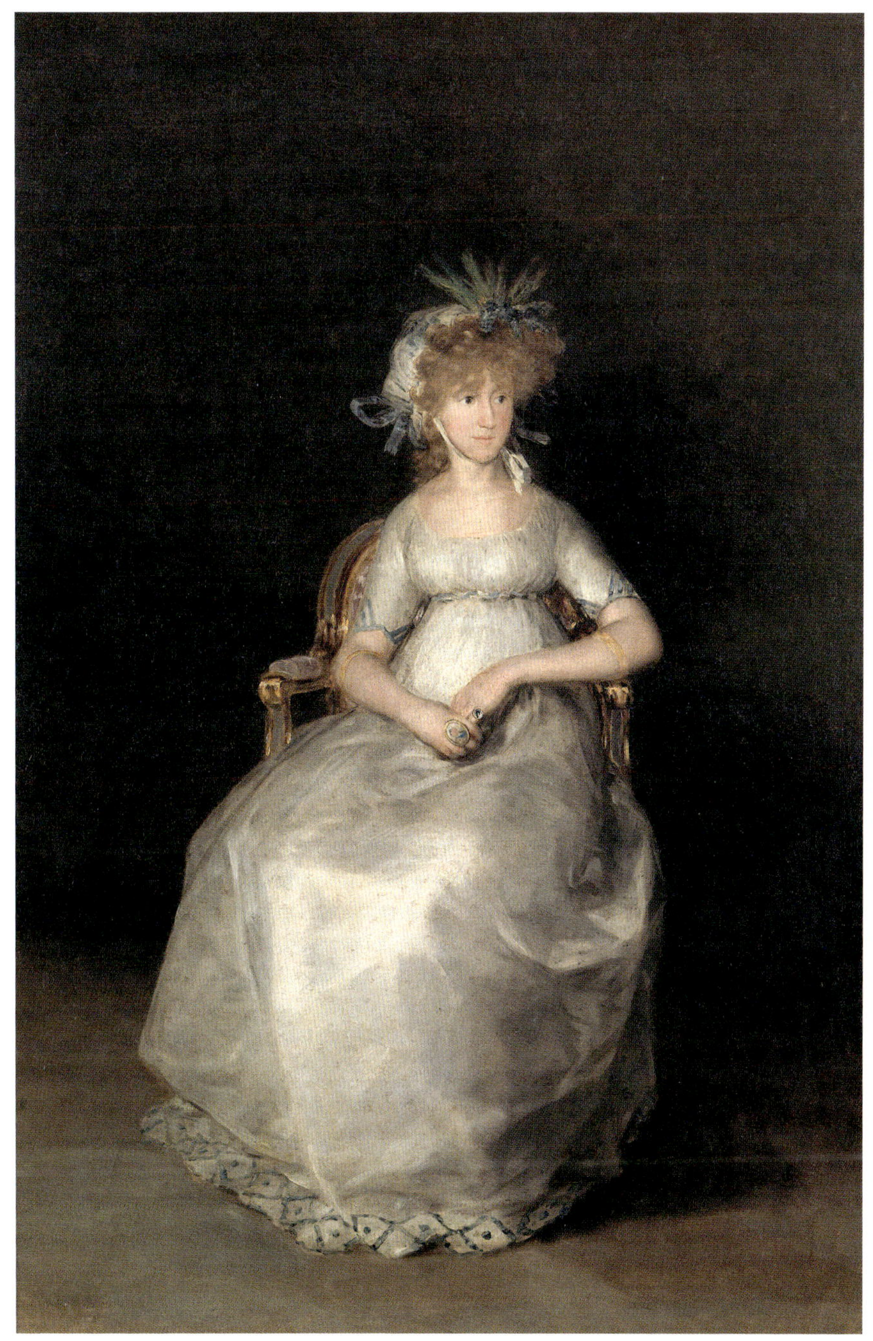

Manuel Godoy, Duke of Alcudia, "Prince of Peace", 1801

Oil on canvas
180 x 267 cm
San Fernando Royal Academy of Fine Arts, Madrid

Painted in August and September of 1801, this portrait, turned untraditionally on its side, provides us with a slightly ridiculous counterpart to *The Naked Maja* (pages 72/73). Captain General Godoy, at the peak of his power, reclines not on a bed but on a field commander's chair which looks as if it is about to break under his weight. This portly man, whose yellow trousers are ill-fitting and whose battle gear reflects the so called War of the Oranges, led that brief skirmish where the French and Spanish fought against the Portuguese who had refused to accept Napoleon's demands to become a political and economic extension of France. The intertwined flags, the aide behind Godoy and the smoky battle raging in the background all celebrate the three-week campaign after which he is said to have picked oranges. He was hailed as a "Prince of Peace" for his part in the Treaty of Basel—the king sent him a letter which he is holding in his hand.
With his tight jacket, feathered hat on the ground and bright trousers he does not look like a prince who has led soldiers into battle and, at the risk of appearing indecent, surely the stick between his legs must be Goya's joke and phallic reference to Godoy's numerous mistresses and his so-called sexual magnetism. Not a point Godoy might even in fact have minded, and certainly he continued to be an excellent patron to Goya.

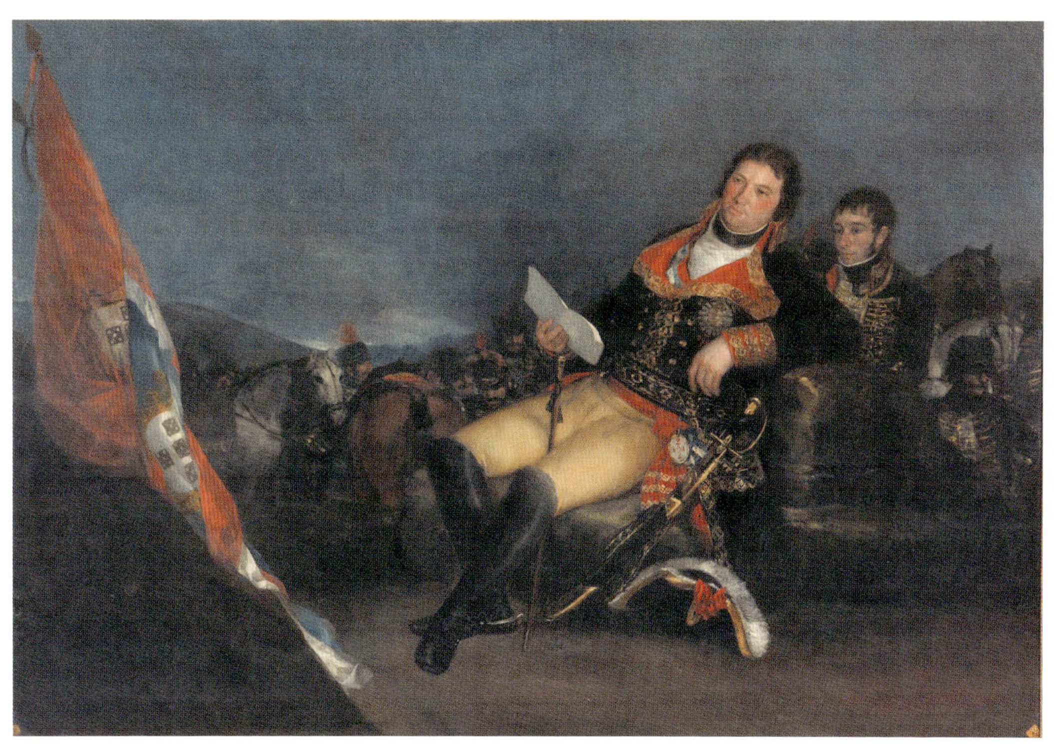

Still Life of Sheep's Ribs and Head (A Butcher's Counter), c. 1808–1812

Oil on canvas
45 x 62 cm
Louvre, Paris

In the long tradition of Spanish still-life painting, this work could be compared with Rembrandt or Soutine, but it is unlikely Goya had encountered Rembrandt's work and Soutine was not yet born. Did he know Zurbaran's spectacular *Agnus Dei* (1635–40), a merino sheep, with its legs bound, lying flat on a larder counter, trussed, dead, Christ-like, too pathetic for anyone to think of eating it? Somehow it tugs at our humanity.

Against a black background Goya has propped one rack of mutton against another and they take centre stage in this chilling indictment of cruelty. Meat has been hacked off the animal and the indifference of the butcher's knife can actually be felt—it's a job and nothing more. There is no desire to eat evoked here. It is a reminder of the cruel act of death as so many died on the Spanish fields and would die again a century later. The dull and lifeless eyes of the sheep on the left watch its own slaughter. One tiny protruding tooth juts out of its mouth, suggesting the act of chewing, but this decapitated animal stands instead for all those who have lost their lives in the futile wars. The meat is not edible, it is a carcass, it is strewn and has no dignity.

So disturbed, so angry was Goya that he could hardly bare to sign this work. On careful examination, a tiny signature in red, as if in blood in the shadows under the head, can be detected.

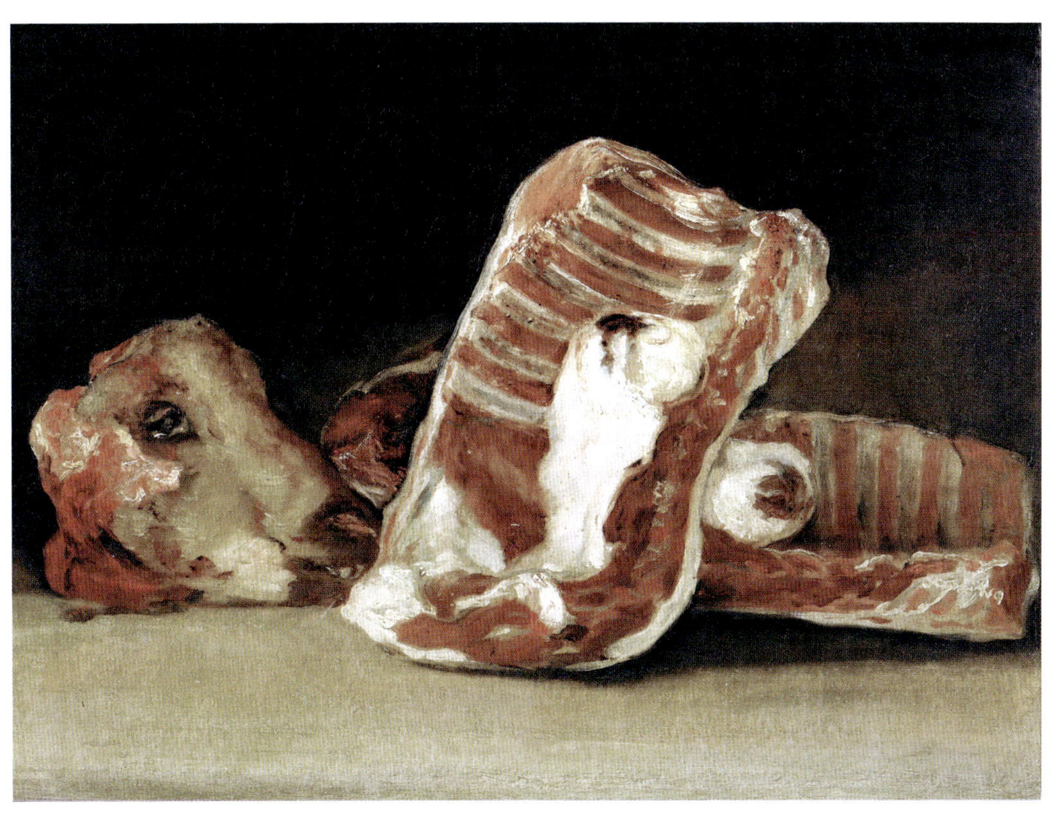

The Colossus, c. 1810–12

Oil on canvas
116 x 102 cm
Museo del Prado, Madrid

The Napoleonic Wars had been raging since 1803 but now the First French Empire turned its attention to Spain. In 1807 the Spanish king and queen had been duped into leaving their country and were in exile in France. By 1808 the new king, Ferdinand VII, was forced to abdicate and the so-called Peninsular War began. Independence from French rule proved long and bloody but the tenacious Spaniards, whose armies were ill-equipped and small, eventually won in 1814, when Ferdinand took back the throne. Godoy, infatuated with Napoleon, had facilitated the entry of the French army into Spain. Now, without the support of the Bourbon king and queen, he was detained, and Joseph Bonaparte, Napoleon's older brother, put on the Spanish crown. A turbulent time began in Goya's life as can be seen in the next few works.

The date of this painting is uncertain although listed in inventories as 1812. It can best be placed during the wars, its original title being *The Giant* and later *Panic*. The boxer in the centre of the painting could be Napoleon himself; or can this work be understood as an allegory of Spain revolting against Napoleon? It is certainly enigmatic. The figure emerges from the rolling Spanish countryside, perhaps Northern Spain, into the smoke-filled clouds, his eyes tightly shut, his fists at the ready. If this is meant as a personification of Spain, it is an accurate depiction. Spanish soldiers fought by any means and often with no weapons. Here is the start of guerilla warfare. Beneath him people and animals lie dying or dead, fleeing his terrible force—refugees with wagons loaded with possessions who are all too familiar once again today and who are poignant reminders of the impact of war.

There has been much argument about attribution regarding this work. In 2021 the Museo del Prado officially declared that it was indeed by Goya. No doubt academics will continue to debate.

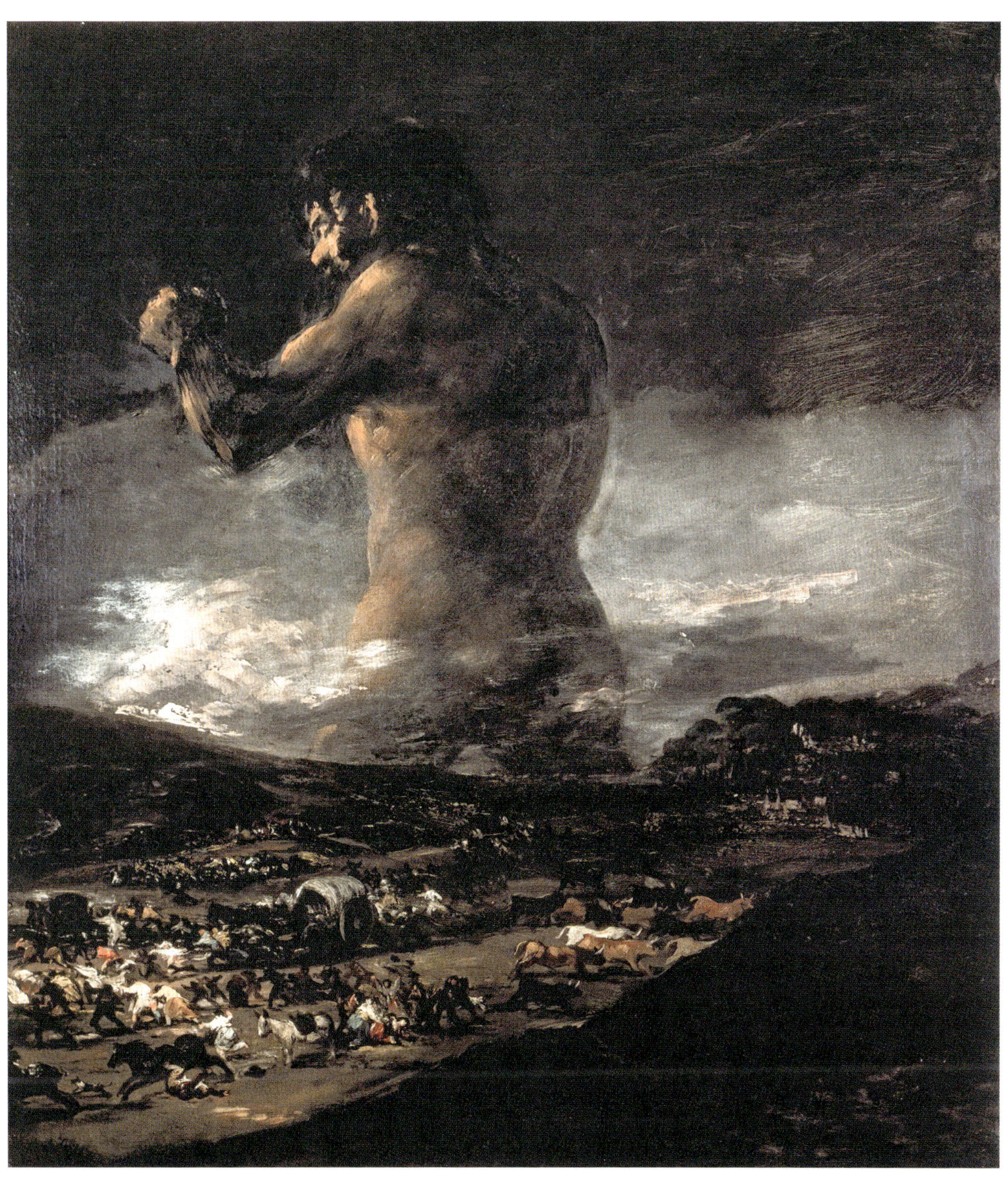

The Disasters of War (Los Desastres de la Guerra): "What Courage!" (Qué valor!), c. 1810–15 (etching), 1863 (publication)

Etching and aquatint
15.2 x 21.5 cm
The Metropolitan Museum of Art, New York

Between 2 and 8 October 1808 Goya returned to his native Zaragoza where he would find patriotic Aragonese men and women fighting and defending their territory against the French during the siege of the city. Goya records some of the scenes in oils—which were difficult to get hold of during wartime—especially the everyday acts of heroism of ordinary people. This work is part of his series called *The Disasters of War*, which were done in aquatint at a time when copper was scarce. He did not use multiple working proofs, partly for economic reasons, but also to highlight the immediacy of these tableaus of suffering, hunger and death. Goya probably did not see the event, which is depicted here, directly as it happened on 15 June 1808, but he certainly heard about it afterwards. A young Zaragozan woman called Agustina Raimunda María Saragossa I Domènech was said to have looked for an opportunity to engage in war. She had clambered over dead bodies near the ramparts of the city to fire a twenty-six-pound cannon at the advancing French soldiers. Legends like to elaborate a good story—her lover was apparently one of those slain corpses; a fact that might have further fuelled her anger.

This powerful etching displays Goya's obvious admiration for the patriots, and his addition 'What courage', further emphasises his thinking. The composition is in perfect symmetry. The pyramidal structure of a hill in the distance and the mound of corpses are offset by the round wheel of the cannon which juts out into the skyline. The black and white of the etching allows Goya to highlight Agustina's slender body as well as the tip of the cannon, along with the shirts of the men and their bare legs in white, and her little hand which holds the match. Her fragility, her feminine nape, breast and hint of her buttocks are all arranged so as not to excite the senses but as a sign that bravery was also to be found in the souls of women during the wars. Goya highlights this in many of his eighty-two *Disasters of War* which were made between 1810 and 1815 and not published by the Academia de San Fernando until 1863. Were they just too brutal to publish before?

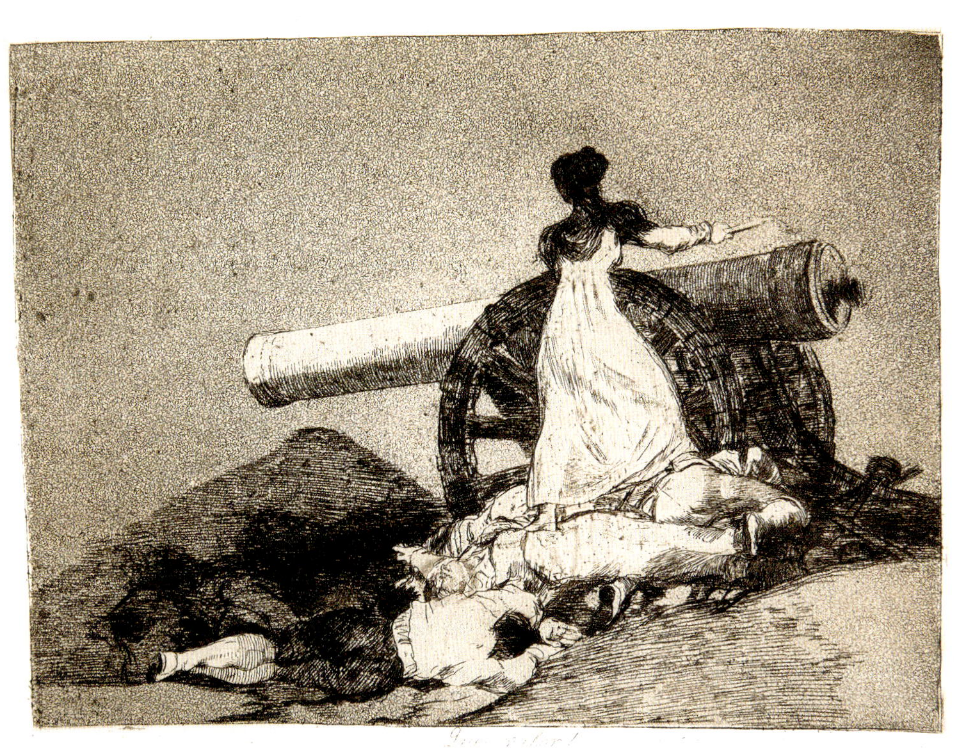

The Duke of Wellington, 1812–14

Oil on mahogany panel
64.3 x 52.4 cm
The National Gallery, London

How do you paint your saviour? Arthur Wellesley, a leading political figure
and statesman, had been British Prime Minister twice. By 1808 he began his
participation in the Peninsular War to fight against Napoleon with the Spanish
and the Portuguese. He arrived in Lisbon in 1809, secured Portugal and then
began his campaign in Spain, which included important battles at Badajoz,
Arapiles near Salamanca, Victoria and finally at Waterloo, where he famously
encountered Napoleon and defeated him. Napoleon abdicated on 13 April
1813. The now Duke of Wellington was made a Spanish Grandee and hailed
a conquering hero on 3 May 1814. The War of Spanish Independence against
Napoleon was over. Goya was to capture his likeness three times—once in a
small red chalk drawing (page 27) which was perhaps a study for this work.
In this oil portrait painted on mahogany, the duke appears to come out of the
penumbra that surrounds him; he stares wide-eyed and alert at the artist or
viewer, his face slightly flushed. The angle of his head suggests pride both for
his campaign and also for being Goya's subject. But he also looks exhausted
with a five o'clock shadow which contrasts magnificently with the red of his
uniform. Its various pinks, blues, yellows and reds display a subtle brilliance.
The duke bears an impressive array of medals, both Spanish and English—the
Peninsular medal was established specifically for the Napoleonic Wars, but
the more prestigious Order of the Golden Fleece dated back to 1430 and was
conferred on Wellington in 1812, making him the first protestant to receive that
honour.

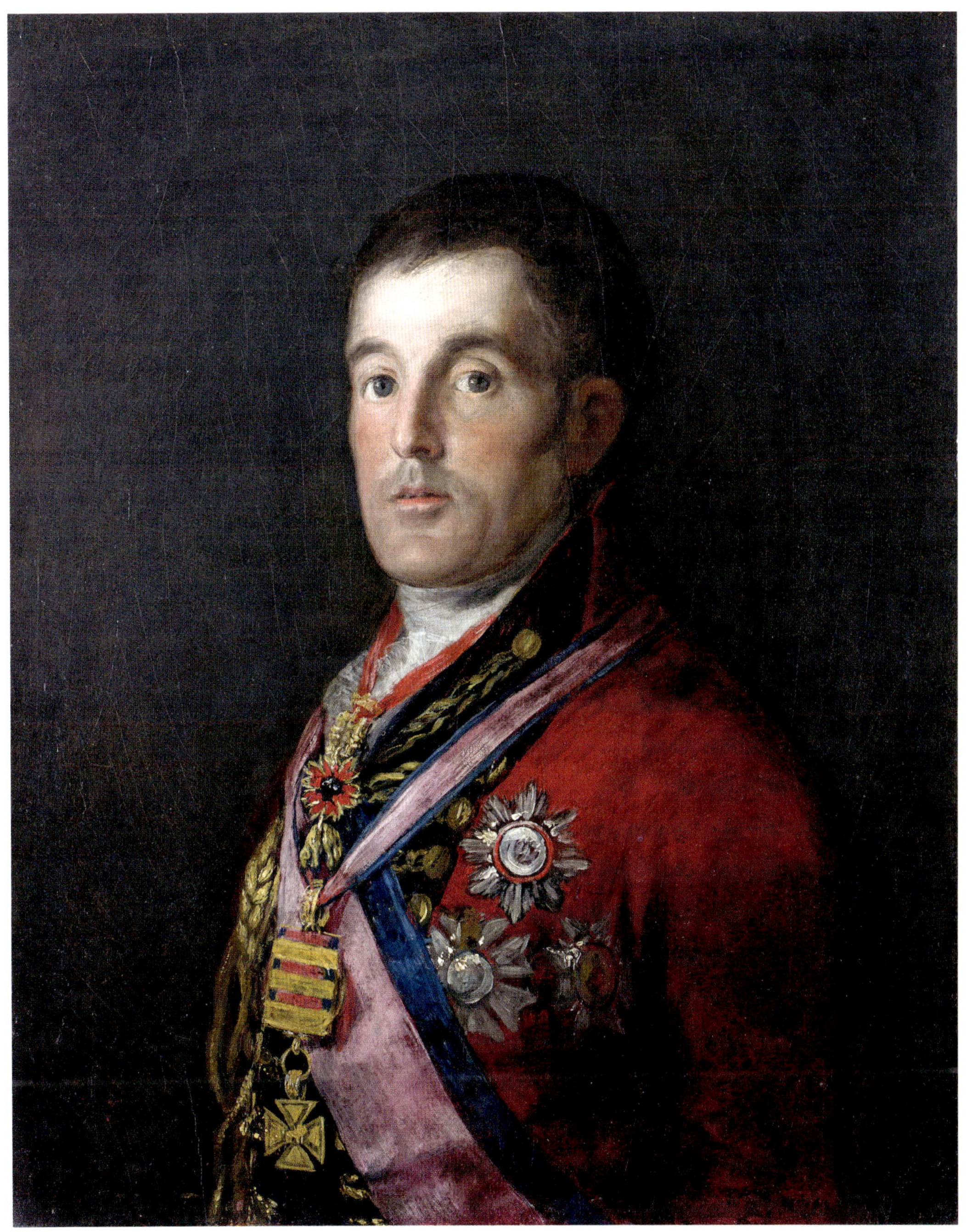

The 3rd of May 1808 in Madrid, 1814

Oil on canvas
266 x 345 cm
Museo del Prado, Madrid

This painting, executed to commemorate a gruesome event which happened six years earlier, is part of a pair, the earlier one called 2 May 1808 (pages 32/33). Both are of impressive size and were clearly meant to be seen by the public. The two hang together in the Prado. Goya's own position during and after the Peninsular War was precarious. He had possibly supported the French Revolutionary aims and was perhaps *afrancesado* (pro French), mainly because he did not wish to see the downfall of Spain. He was horrified by the atrocities which might have been avoided if Spain had accepted French rule. But the events that took place on 2 May when the mob revolted against the French cuirassiers and the Mamelukes—who were North Africans—at the Puerta del Sol in Madrid was going to have reprisals. And it is these which provide the overwhelming story for this painting.
Men were rounded up and taken either to the Prince Pio Hill or the Buen Retiro park, where they were shot at point blank range by heavily-clad, faceless, robotic French soldiers who lean forward in their zealous drive for revenge. The scene takes place at nighttime but is lit by an oil lamp, as if staged to allow the viewer to witness the horror of the scene—one which would resonate with artists such as Manet or Picasso centuries later. There are three stages of death depicted here. The sheer fear and terror of those who face their demise imminently or look away; the extraordinary bravery of the rugged Christlike figure who accepts his choiceless fate; and those who have already gone through death's door and lie in their own and each other's encrusted blood on the ground. It is a hymn to all of the fallen soldiers—a commemoration of bravery; the painting was commissioned by Ferdinand VII, and Goya equates their courage with unwilling martyrdom. The central figure with his arms outstretched
and the stigmata on his hands, stands for the cause of freedom. In his white shirt and yellow trousers in front of the blood-red of his fellow men one cannot help but see the colours of the Spanish flag only then recently adopted in 1785.

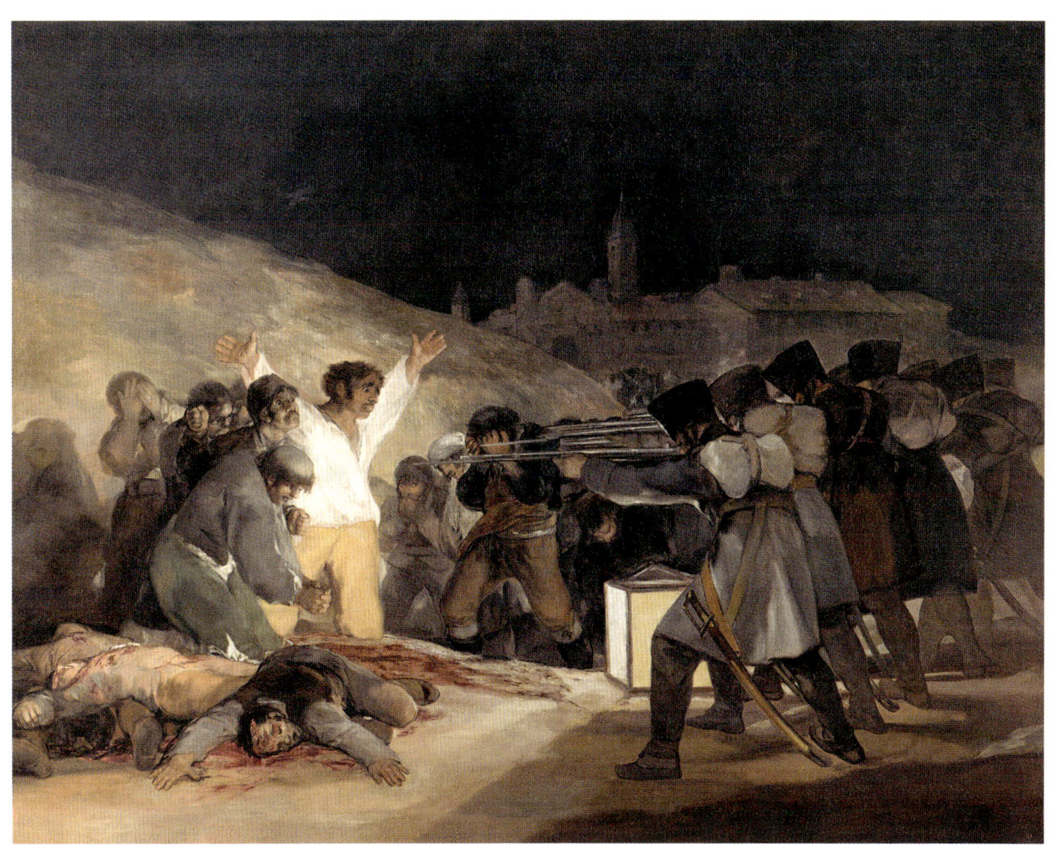

Ferdinand VII in Court Dress, 1814/15

Oil on canvas
207 x 140 cm
Museo del Prado, Madrid

There was no love lost between the new King Ferdinand VII and Goya, but after the wars he returned to his duty as court painter of the monarchs. As a despotic and absolutist monarch of rigid principles Ferdinand VII might just have been one of the worst kings Spain had ever seen. He waged war against the *afrancesados* (those he saw as conspirators with the French) and liberals. Having just rejected the liberal constitution of 1812, Ferdinand is holding a mantle beside the handle of his gilded sword leaving the viewer in no doubt of his power. With his other hand he grips the sceptre, equally a symbol of his power on the throne he has stolen from his father. So how does Goya show displeasure with the man he will soon flee from, in a full-length royal portrait which the king was said to have been pleased with? Goya had to beg for sittings and was eventually granted two, each of forty-five minutes. In some ways this is crucial to an understanding of Goya's paintings. There is no satire here or humorous take on this swaggering man. There really was very little to laugh about during his reign. What had he done for Spain in its time of need? The answer surely lies in the juxtaposition between the fine regalia in all its glory and lavish details; the brocaded velvet-red cloak with fur line trimmings, the medal on his chest of the Golden Fleece together with the blue sash, blue trousers with a golden hem and the gold-buckled shoes which look too small—all that finery on a portly man with a head perhaps a tad too small, a slightly leering smile spreading on his too fat cheeks and a twisted angle of the head, offset to the left as if he had just seen Goya, not really posed for him. The artist has captured his magnificence with all the trappings to remind us of how important he was, yet he looks uncomfortable and ill at ease under the painter's brush. Goya had not been salaried under the rule of Joseph Bonaparte, which saved him now, and this portrait was executed to show his loyalty to the new Spanish king.

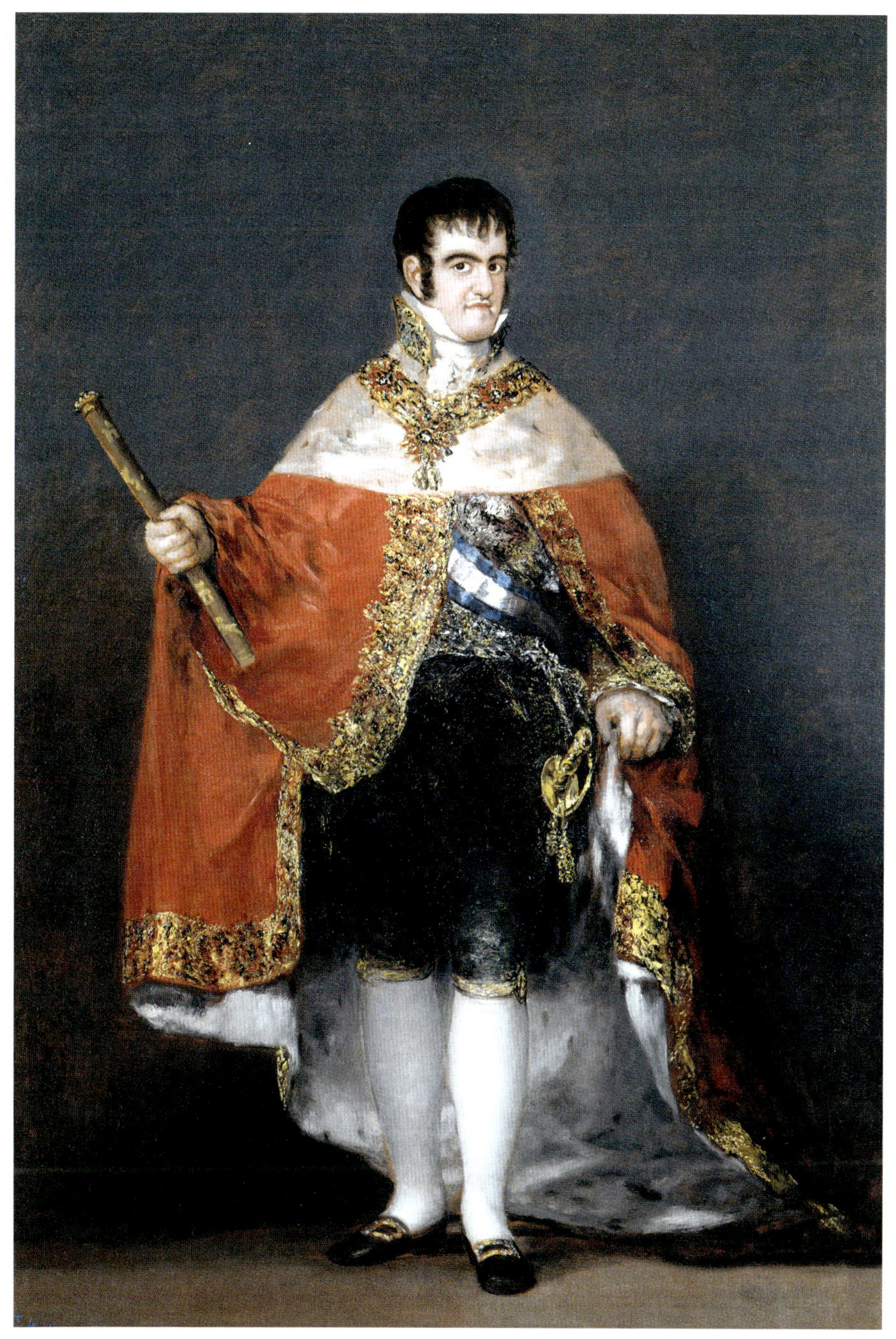

The Bullfight, 1814–16

Oil on panel
45 x 72 cm
San Fernando Royal Academy of Fine Arts, Madrid

In his letters Goya mentions bullfighting and it can be assumed that he would have attended at least one bullfight and have known some of the famous figures of the time personally. On pages 60/61 we see him wearing a bullfighter's jacket, he even claimed he had fought bulls when he was young. An unfounded brag a few Spaniards might make.

The Disasters of War had certainly left him exhausted, so in 1815/16 he embarked on a new series of *Tauromachia (The Art of Bullfighting)* to commemorate the age-old Spanish tradition of pitting bull and man in front of a crowd of braying onlookers. Some see the spectacle as a metaphor for life, some for death; many played out in the numerous bullrings of Spain and others on makeshift ones which popped up in the smaller villages which couldn't afford anything else, like the one here. In the *Tauromachia* etchings Goya documents the development of the sport and embeds it in Spanish culture without the trappings of fine costumes and neoclassical arenas. This is a popular spectacle for the village, the ring is improvised and the uniformed but anonymous picador, the 'hero' of this piece, performs his expected manoeuvres in front of a rowdy crowd.

There was and is much opposition to this 'sport'—indeed, during Goya's lifetime, in 1785 and 1805 by royal decree, bulls were not killed. But as Spain emerged bruised and battered from the Peninsular War, there was a conservative call for the revival of typically Spanish traditions. Some saw bullfighting as a metaphor for Spain's backwardness, others as a diversion for the people; for those who had survived the war, mostly men, they could continue to fight or more often to watch. This scene is uncontrolled and dangerous; horses are unprotected, and toreros seem to be brawling. The action is incredibly close to the crowd who have come out of their houses to observe and witness the ritual.

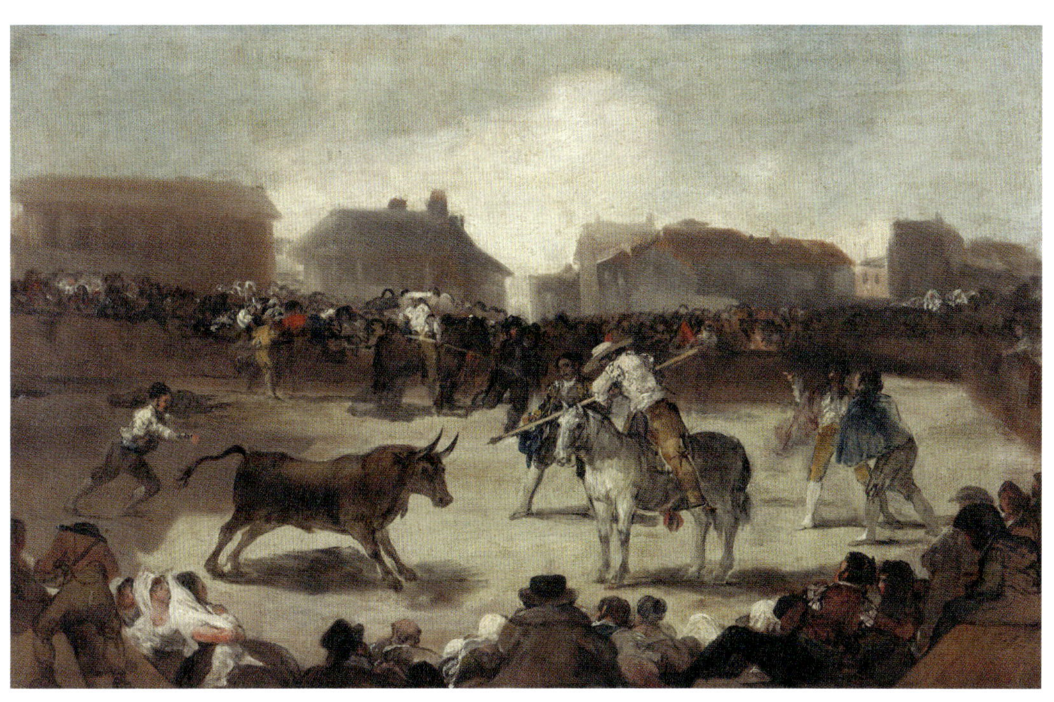

Self-Portrait, 1815

Oil on canvas
46 x 35 cm
Museo del Prado, Madrid

With this life-sized study of the artist's head cocked on one side and his hair more untamed than ever, Goya shows us a face in conflict, half in shadow—there are no signs of décor and no elaborate clothes. The modelled face has a sense of fleshiness and three-dimensionality. This self-portrait is evidence of fear and suffering; humanity laid bare. It has seen the French invasion at first hand. Goya is sixty-nine and weary. His eyes disappear into their sockets and he is so close to the picture plane that you can almost smell him; smell the sweat of hard work. This is not the court painter Goya, this is Goya working, painting as he has always done, to faithfully render what he sees—in this case, his own face in the mirror, warts and all. The war has ended but his own personal war has not. Soon he will make the decision to leave court but for now he is caught in a melancholy mood. Goya has produced a number of important works thus far but a purification process has begun to clear him of collaboration with the French king, and the Inquisition have begun sniffing around asking questions about "a naked woman on a bed", (pages 72/73)—the outcome of which is unclear, but Goya survives unscathed. The portrait is signed on the lower left—"Fr. Goya Pintor, Aragonese, by himself, 1815"—almost as if it acts as a last will and testament, a statement to the viewer to remember him and his roots.

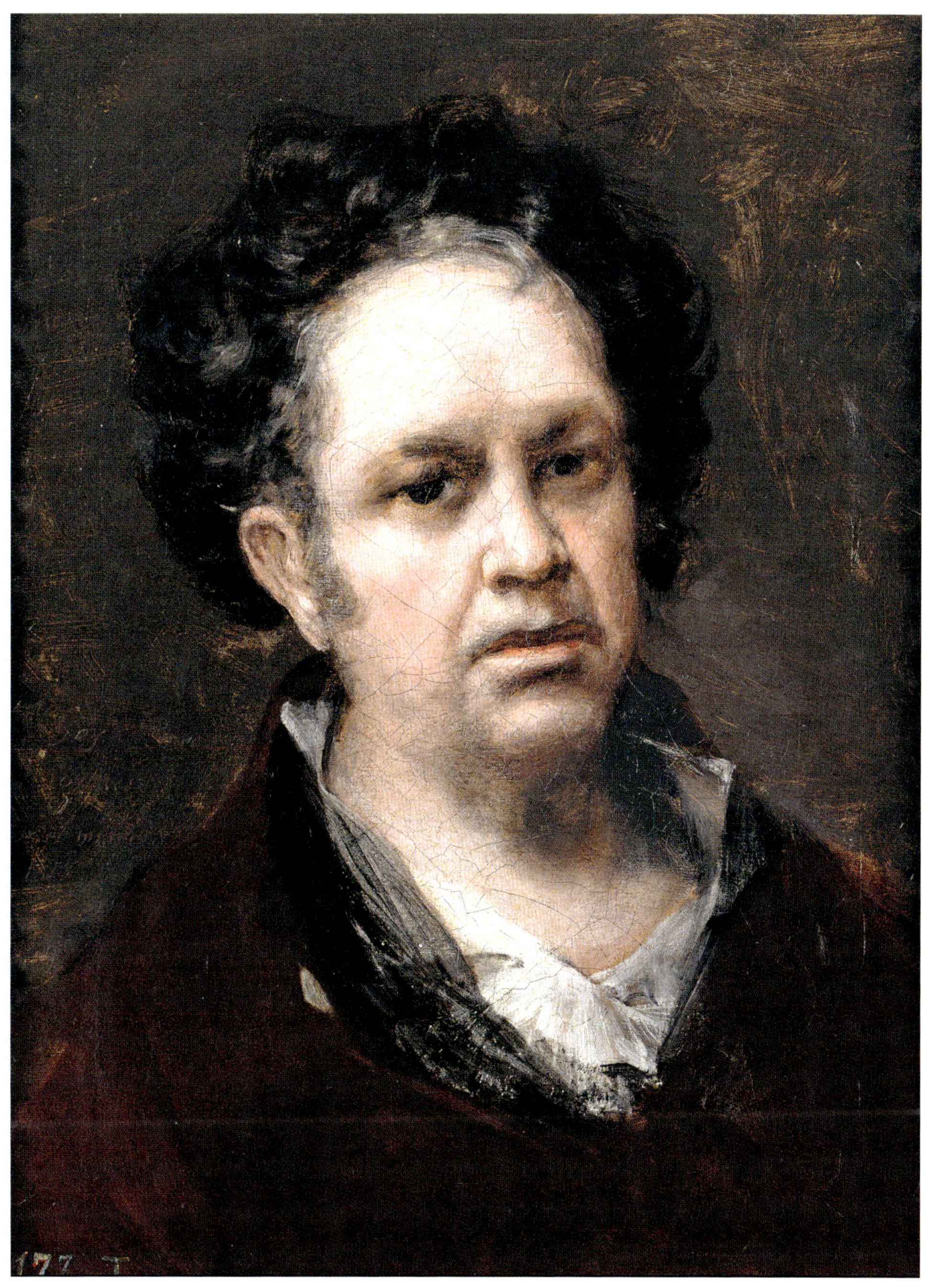

Inquisition Scene, 1816

Oil on panel
46 x 73 cm
San Fernando Royal Academy of Fine Arts, Madrid

The Spanish Inquisition was eventually abolished in 1834, six years after Goya's death. During his lifetime it was abolished by Joseph Bonaparte but became central again to Fernando VII's rule and the restoration of the Spanish monarchy, setting Spain apart from the rest of Europe. Barbaric and cruel to the extreme, the practice of execution gradually waned and the weeding out of non-Catholics was exchanged for the persecution of heretics, libertines and *afrancesados* who were all seen as subversive elements in a nervous Spain which still remembered the French Revolution.
Here we witness an *auto-da-fé* which was a ceremony of sentencing convicted prisoners. Often 'celebrated' outdoors, where a crowd could be whipped up, this one is inside. Instead of the public, various monastic orders can be seen—the Dominicans, the Capuchins and the Franciscans—all identifiable by their habits. There are four prisoners wearing the capirote hat and yellow tunics decorated with flames, dragons and devils. The repenting only wore the flames. The bowed figures are highlighted by the golden light Goya casts across the painting. He is documenting a possible scene and avoiding a sympathetic eye—instead we are faced with the power of repression. The preacher's closed eyes suggest he declaims a text he knows well; the victims are hemmed in not just by the authority of the church, represented by one large pillar, but also by the architecture of the room which affords no escape.
What Goya cannot overtly paint is there in its absence. Nearly four hundred years of oppression by all the monastic orders and those who chose to abuse power. This is social commentary as was the previous image, but carefully rendered to avoid conflict.

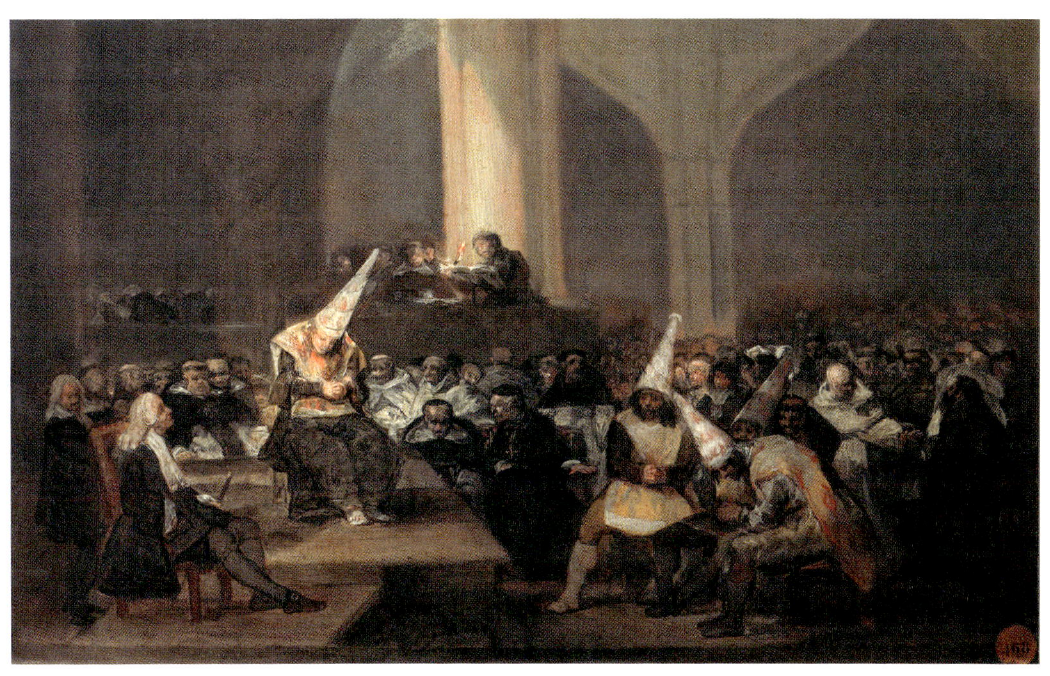

Judith and Holofernes, c. 1819–23

Oil mural transferred to canvas
144 x 82 cm
Museo del Prado, Madrid

What frame of mind Goya was in when he decamped with a woman called Leocadia Weiss, née Zorrilla, (his wife had died in 1812) to a dilapidated house near the river Manzanares, which he had acquired in February 1819, we will never really know. He had been through several illnesses, lived with deafness for many years, seen off two kings, lived uncomfortably with a third—Fernando VII—and witnessed the horrors of the Peninsular War all too closely. Goya's world was darkened by the time he moved. To leave court and set up home just across the Segovia Bridge, where he had bought a house ironically called *The House of the Deaf Man*, must have been an enormous upheaval in his seventies.

Why he set about painting the walls of this house is also a mystery. However it is known that there were fourteen pictures arranged over two floors in the house, although even that fact is sometimes disputed. Photographs taken by Jean Laurent in 1874 show that they were painted over existing works, on top of wallpaper and then framed. It is interesting to observe that Goya knew the art of fresco mural painting, as seen on pages 76/77, yet after sizing these walls in sulphur and calcium, he chooses oil paint mixed with sand. Were they ever meant to last and be seen by others or were they the demented outpourings of a man who was ill, poisoned by the lead in his paintings and traumatised by what he had witnessed? It is also possible that he had a good deal of fun buttering his walls in paint and that they are an example of his new-found freedom. The answer remains unknown but, thanks to their removal off the walls and transference to canvas in 1872/73 for the 1878 Exhibition Universelle, they can since be seen.

Goya had approached the theme of Judith and Holofernes earlier in his career but this seemingly nighttime version with its raw blacks, ochres and reds laid on thickly and energetically, captures the biblical story when Judith, a Jewish widow, seduces and then murders the Assyrian general Holofernes to save her town of Bethulia. Goya had previously depicted the bravery of women in the wars (pages 90/91) but this is done with a blood curdling roar of energy.

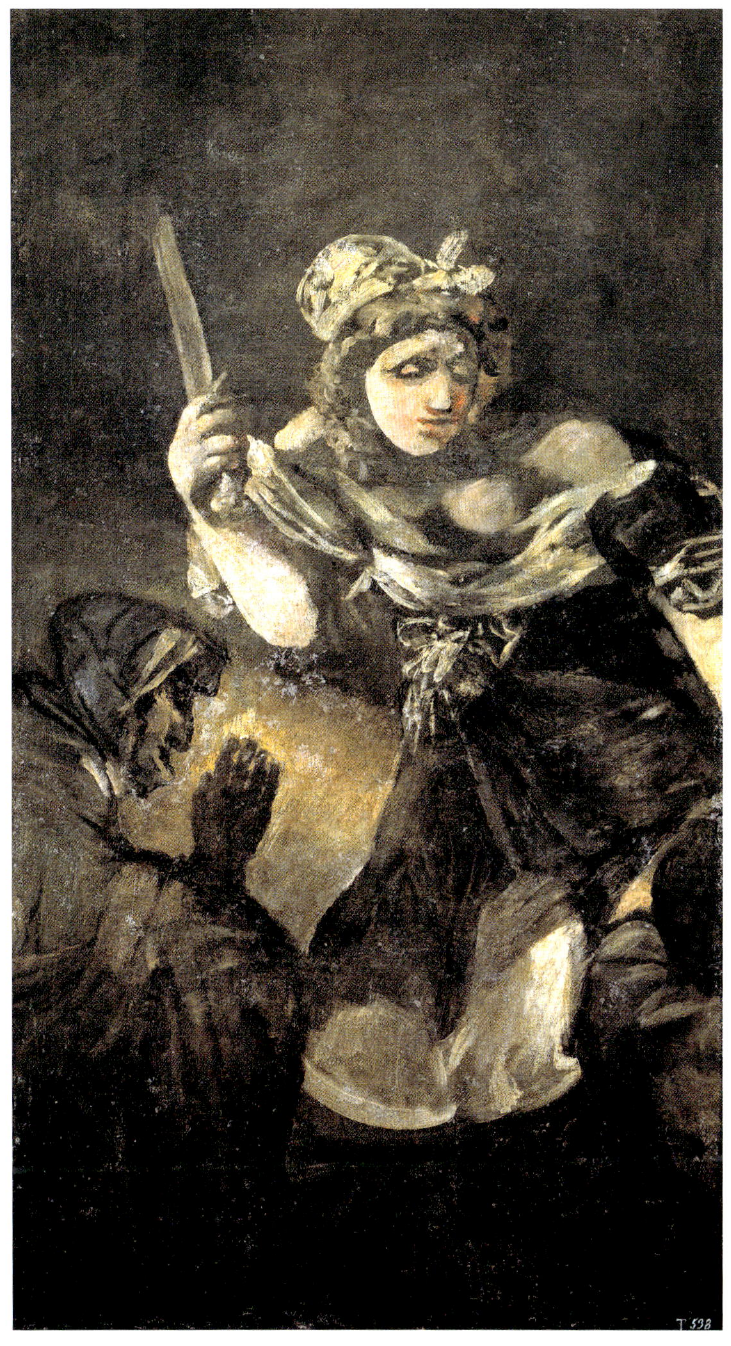

Self-Portrait with Dr Arrieta, 1820

Oil on canvas
116 x 79 cm
Minneapolis Institute of Art

In this work Goya is apparently on his death bed. From Bacchus (pages 80/81) to a sickly weak man surrounded by shadowy representatives of the church or friends and neighbours who are there to witness the moment. The bald inscription reads, "Goya, in gratitude to his friend Arrieta: for the compassion and care with which he saved his life during the acute and dangerous illness he suffered towards the end of the year 1819 in his seventy-third year. He painted this in 1820." Dr Eugenio García Arrieta was one of only two doctors appointed in October 1819 to Madrid's Supreme Council of Health. He is presented here not as a priest protecting Goya, but as an esteemed doctor. Goya seems to be claiming—as was the case—that medicine is emerging from the shadows of the Church. The artist is in green, his symbolic colour of hope, although not as bright a colour as Arrieta the healer wears. Goya's face is partially in shadow to suggest inner contradictions, or perhaps he is half-alive and half-dead. The Pietistic format, the glass filled with wine—or is it medicine?—the crimson blanket and the counterpane he nervously plucks at, all point us iconographically towards some kind of relinquishment or sacrifice. Once Godly, he is now Christ enshrining himself. Goya has finally emerged from the darkness and is stripped of all myth—he is humble, pathetic and near death. Although he is not to die for another eight years, it appears that his journey in self-portraits has finally come to an end. He will paint himself no more.

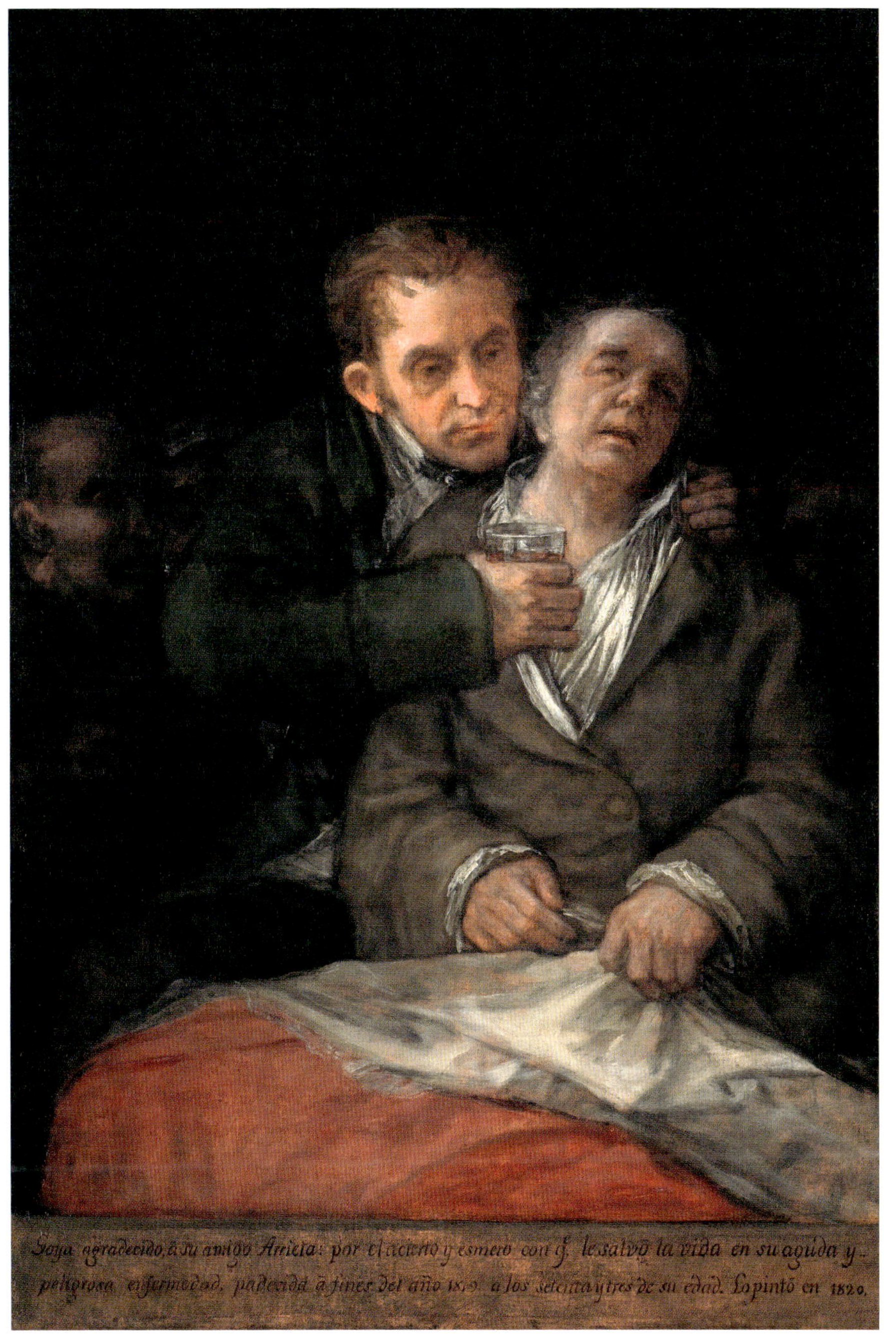
Goya agradecido, á su amigo Arrieta: por el acierto y esmero con q.e le salvó la vida en su aguda y
peligrosa enfermedad, padecida à fines del año 1819, à los setenta y tres de su edad. Lo pintó en 1820.

The Milkmaid of Bordeaux, 1827

Oil on canvas
74 x 68 cm
Museo del Prado, Madrid

Believed to be one of Goya's last works, there is some debate amongst academics over the authenticity of this work. Perhaps this is because we have suddenly been showered with light and colour as if Goya, at just over eighty and now living in exile in Bordeaux, has come to life again. Done just months before his death in 1828, it could be a portrait of Leocadia Weiss who looked after him for many years, or her daughter Rosario. Against a swirling sky, a young woman sits, possibly on a mule, wrapped in a warm shawl with a milk jug either in her right hand, which is not visible, or balanced on the animal. She looks ahead into the far distance as if in thought or in melancholic mood. The work is a symphony in blue; textural and sublime in its muted lighting and atmosphere.

When investigating the left-hand side of the painting, one can see the pentimento—a mark left by an earlier painting that shows where an artist made changes—of a possibly turbaned man looking up at her. The canvas was indeed re-used and X-rays have revealed sketches underneath. As Leocadia's daughter Rosario became Goya's student of painting in 1821, it is perhaps a work done in collaboration. She would go on to paint for many years after Goya's death.

As for this work, it was given to Leocadia who was loathed by Goya's son Javier and who in turn inherited most of his father's estate. At first, she refused to sell it. Then, out of poverty, she did so to one of Goya's relatives, Juan Batista de Muguiro. She told him Goya had urged her to take no less than an ounce of gold for it and he seems to have agreed. The Muguiro family bequeathed it to the Prado in 1946.

Despite his various illnesses and debilitating deafness, Goya lived a long and productive life. He died in Bordeaux at the age of eighty-two, which was very old in those days, on 16 April 1828. In voluntary exile from his native Spain, he continued to record the life around him right up to his death, which was probably caused from an attack of cerebral palsy leaving him partially paralysed. Revolutionary, subversive, humorous and dark he paved the way for generations of artists to come, from Delacroix to Manet, Picasso to Jake and Dinos Chapman and way beyond, encouraging them to express their times freely and bravely. His courageous nature and determination to express the truth in his drawings, paintings and etchings still resonate today.

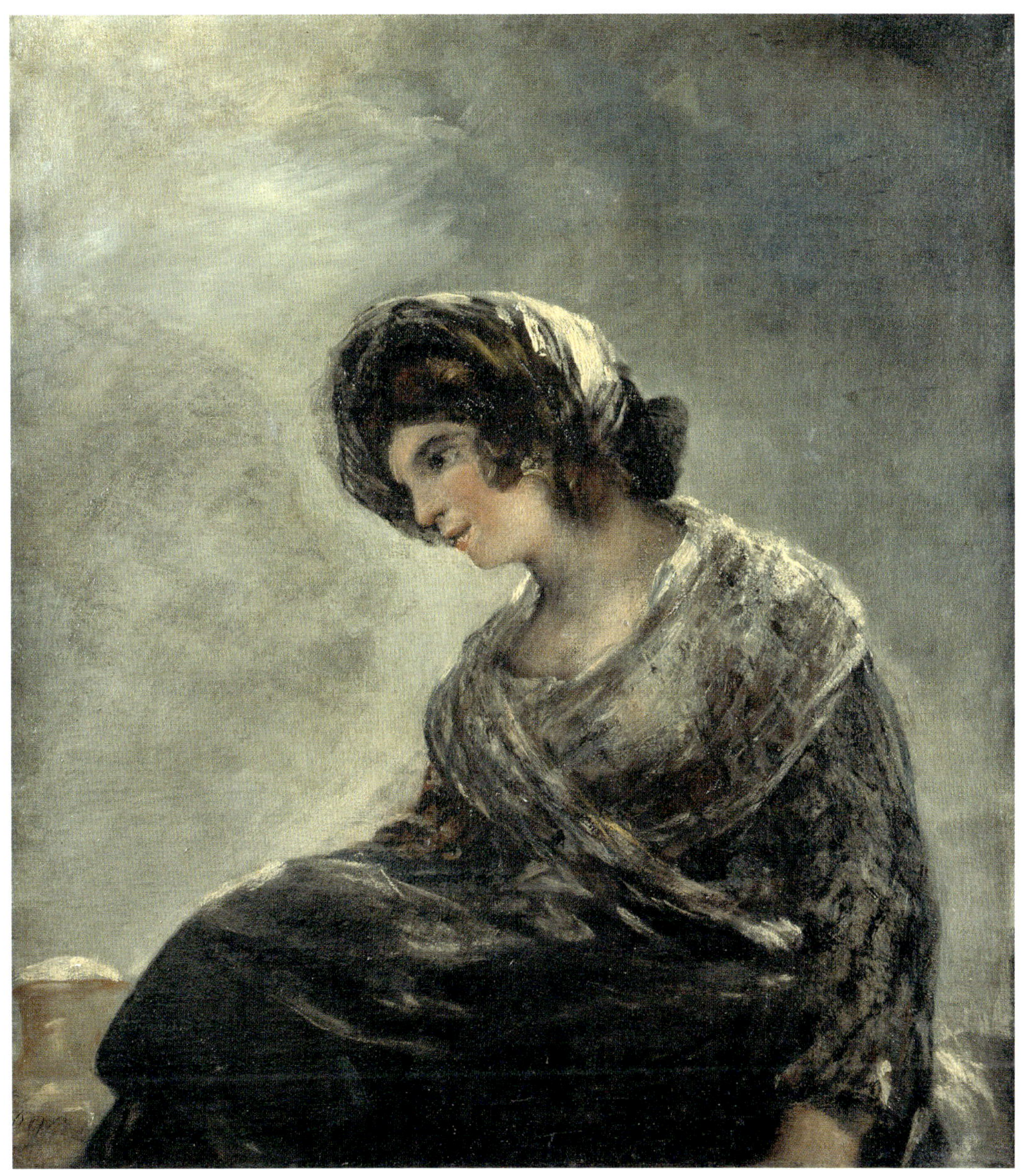

FURTHER READING

Bray, Xavier, and Marqués, B. Mena Manuela, and Gayford, Thomas, *Goya, The Portraits*, New Haven, 2015

Ciofalo, John, *The Self-Portraits of Goya*, Cambridge, 2001

Hughes, Robert, *Goya*, London, 2003

Jordon, William, and Cherry, Peter, *Spanish Still Life from Velázquez to Goya*, New Haven, 1995

Stoichita, Victor, and Coderch, Anne Maria, *Goya, The Last Carnival*, London, 1999

Symmons, Sarah, *Goya*, London, 1998

Symmons, Sarah (ed.), *Goya a Life in Letters*, London, 2004

Tomlinson, Janis, *Goya: A Portrait of the Artist*, New Jersey, 2022

Tomlinson, Janis, *Goya: Images of Women*, New Haven, 2002

Tomlinson, Janis, *Goya in the Twilight of the Enlightenment*, London, 1992

Waldmann, Susanne, *Goya and the Duchess of Alba*, London, 1998

Wilson–Bareau, Juliet, *Goya: Drawings from His Private Albums*, ex.cat., Hayward Gallery, London, 2001

Wolf, Norbert, *Spanish Painting from the Golden Age to Modernism*, London, 2023

PHOTO CREDITS

akg images: 25 (Album / Oronoz); 43, 45 (Erich Lessing); 59 (De Agostini Picture Library); 65 (Heritage Images / Fine Art Images); 87 (Fine Art Images); 89 (Joseph S. Martín

Art Institute of Chicago: 19 (Gift of J. C. Cebrian)

Artothek: 49 (Hans Hinz)

Bridgeman Images: Frontispiece, 61, 103

Metropolitan Museum of Art, New York: 57 (Rogers Fund, 1906); 69 (Gift of M. Knoedler & Co., 1918)

National Gallery of Art, Washington: 14 (Ailsa Mellon Bruce Collection); 34 (Rosenwald Collection)

Wikimedia Commons: Cover, 8/9, 10, 11, 12/13, 17, 18, 20/21, 22, 23, 25, 26, 27, 28/29, 30, 32/33, 35, 37, 38/39, 41, 47, 51, 53, 55, 63, 67, 71, 73, 75, 77, 79, 81, 83, 85, 91, 93, 95, 97, 99, 101, 105, 107, 109